Inside Copilot

Inside Copilot is designed to teach users to master Copilot, Microsoft's generative AI assistant. Learn prompt engineering and use cases for Copilot in many Microsoft products at beginner, intermediate, and expert levels. Perfect for any professionals who find their schedules packed with repetitive computer tasks, Copilot can automatically generate PowerPoint presentations, draft emails on Outlook, write code on GitHub, and more. Both companies and individuals can learn to utilize Copilot to significantly speed up processes and gain an advantage.

More information about this series at https://www.apress.com/series/17432.

Copilot for Microsoft 365

Harness the Power of Generative AI in the Microsoft Apps You Use Every Day

Jess Stratton

Apress®

Copilot for Microsoft 365: Harness the Power of Generative AI in the Microsoft Apps You Use Every Day

Jess Stratton
Charlestown, RI, USA

ISBN-13 (pbk): 979-8-8688-0446-5   ISBN-13 (electronic): 979-8-8688-0447-2
https://doi.org/10.1007/979-8-8688-0447-2

Managing Director, Apress Media LLC: Welmoed Spahr
Acquisitions Editor: Ryan Byrnes
Development Editor: Laura Berendson
Editorial Project Manager: Gryffin Winkler

Cover designed by eStudioCalamar

Distributed to the book trade worldwide by Springer Science+Business Media New York, 1 New York Plaza, Suite 4600, New York, NY 10004-1562, USA. Phone 1-800-SPRINGER, fax (201) 348-4505, e-mail orders-ny@springer-sbm.com, or visit www.springeronline.com. Apress Media, LLC is a California LLC and the sole member (owner) is Springer Science + Business Media Finance Inc (SSBM Finance Inc). SSBM Finance Inc is a **Delaware** corporation.

For information on translations, please e-mail booktranslations@springernature.com; for reprint, paperback, or audio rights, please e-mail bookpermissions@springernature.com.

Apress titles may be purchased in bulk for academic, corporate, or promotional use. eBook versions and licenses are also available for most titles. For more information, reference our Print and eBook Bulk Sales web page at http://www.apress.com/bulk-sales.

Any source code or other supplementary material referenced by the author in this book is available to readers on GitHub. For more detailed information, please visit https://www.apress.com/gp/services/source-code.

If disposing of this product, please recycle the paper

This book is dedicated to my late father Joseph Spinosa, one of the OG technical writers, and my mother Annthea, who despite being a true scholar of continuous learning will valiantly follow along even though she doesn't use Copilot and that's what makes her amazing.

Also, to my wonderful and brilliant colleagues Marjorie Page and Toby Malina, who introduced me to Copilot and patiently made it possible to learn and explore the brand-new technology together while it was turbulent and still in development.

Finally, to Dr. Joan Peckham, my computer science professor at URI and my OG STEM hero.

Table of Contents

About the Author

Jess Stratton (a.k.a. Nerd Girl Jess) is a tech trainer, productivity expert, and former senior staff instructor with lynda.com/LinkedIn Learning. With over 50 published courses in the LinkedIn Learning library and thousands of hours of live teaching and webinars, she specializes in Microsoft 365, productivity, and the Google Workspace suite of products. Her courses on Excel have over one million views on LinkedIn Learning, and some have even been featured on Delta's in-flight entertainment systems. She has owned and operated a successful brick-and-mortar boutique style computer learning facility and currently has a podcast titled Nerd Girl Jess Untangles Tech. You can find her at nerdgirljess.com.

About the Technical Reviewer

Zewei Song is a developer, support engineer, consultant, and architect who resides in the Chicagoland area. He holds a Ph.D. in control engineering and several professional certifications, such as Certified ScrumMaster, Microsoft Certified Master, Trainer, and Cybersecurity Architect Expert, just to name a few.

Zewei has many years of experience in consulting, proactive support, and technical advisory. He worked for Microsoft for almost 17 years as a senior consultant and field engineer and then joined Discover Financial Services, taking on the role of senior manager in charge of their Microsoft 365 portfolio. Now, Zewei is set to embark on a new journey with Invoke, LLC as a cloud solution architect, where his focus will be on Microsoft Copilot and Purview solutions.

Zewei's aim through work is to be a leader/influencer who helps enterprises maximize their technology investments and enhance end users' productivity. He is happily married and has two kids. He likes to go bicycling and do photography in his spare time.

Acknowledgments

Special thanks to Samara Iodice, Misty Teach-McCloud, and the incredible assets team at my previous workplace for giving me invaluable experience so I could set up my own demo accounts and real-world content for teaching. I do try to ensure that my fictional accounts are not overscheduled though I *am* working on giving them additional hobbies besides coffee breaks and lunchtime walks. Tell Jenny Torres and Leslie Richardson I miss them dearly.

Introduction

When Copilot was announced, it caused a bit of a furor. This new generative artificial intelligence (AI) technology we had been using for about a year to help us be more efficient could now do the same thing in our work environment and directly related to our active work projects. It was – to put it simply – *astounding*. Over the next few months, that furor would turn into more excitement with a side dish of befuddlement. Information posted on the Internet was outdated within weeks. Articles posted without a date were useless. We began speculating in earnest. There wasn't a day in the news without generative AI making *some* sort of headline. Many of you recognized the technology was clearly here to stay yet hadn't had any experience using it. You may still have not yet had a chance to explore what it's all about and what it can do for you.

Fear not, my friend. I'm going to take you through *everything*, and we are starting at the *beginning*. Generative AI is here to stay, and you don't want to be left behind.

You might not know anything and that's OK. I'm glad you're here. You'll be all caught up soon.

The book begins with a few introductory chapters, starting with the history of generative AI. Chapter 1 begins the journey with a quick introduction on some early uses of artificial intelligence in software applications. I'll discuss OpenAI and why it was so integral to the rapid pace of generative AI we are seeing today, what a large language model is and how it's trained, and how to construct a basic and more advanced prompt.

Chapter 2 contains more integral backstory into Microsoft's history of including artificial intelligence into its Office suite of products and how that evolved into Copilot. I'll also deep dive here into the pieces, parts, and processes of Copilot and how they work together to securely answer questions about your organization's data.

Chapter 3 is the last introductory chapter, containing a short but necessary discussion on responsible AI – what it is, what it entails, and what developers are doing to build trust in their artificial intelligence systems. The goal of this chapter is to help alleviate any fears you may have about using AI and to discuss some risks that come from creating and using it.

Chapter 4 contains the specific details on how you can finally get your hands on Copilot. While this book is very specifically about Copilot for Microsoft 365 in an enterprise environment, I will tell you what *all* the available Copilot options are for the core apps, how to get it, what it will cost, and how to verify your apps have the functionality. It's important to note here that while I do talk about licensing, this is not a book for administrators, so I won't be discussing group policies or enabling Copilot across an organization.

Chapters 5–10 are about how to use Copilot with practical examples in the core apps you use every day – Word, Excel, PowerPoint, Outlook, Teams, and Microsoft Graph-grounded chat. I'll show you each app thoroughly, complete with screenshots and prompts so you can get started using Copilot yourself immediately. Here's where you'll see the scope and magnitude of how much it can help you in your daily professional work life. The goal here is to get you excited and eager to start using it right away in your environment.

Finally, Chapter 11 contains a quick conclusion on the sweeping integration of Copilot into the entire Microsoft ecosystem. Copilot will be integrated into just about every Microsoft application soon, including Windows, GitHub, and Sales, to name a few. Copilot is an all-encompassing brand, and while it's expanding into separate Microsoft products, at the very core will always be the Microsoft 365 products that are used daily by millions of people all over the globe.

Try, try, try. Ask Copilot anything and everything. Don't worry, it will all make sense by the end of this book.

CHAPTER 1

An Introduction to Chat and Generative AI

In 1999, Santa Monica-based company LAUNCH Media Inc. released one of the first of its kind: a new Internet music streaming service. In 2001, LAUNCH Media was purchased by Yahoo! for 12 million dollars to integrate its services and create a wider reaching streaming service, LaunchCast. When it was released, users could listen to a song, rate it on a 1–10 scale, and the service would pick more songs to play. Users could skip a song or rate it, and that choice would be stored with that song to form a complex algorithm that would allow the app to choose the next song for a listener based on similar tastes of other listeners. I used it daily while I worked. It enabled me to be exposed to a whole new library of songs I would never have been exposed to otherwise, and this was an all-day, everyday listening experience for me. As far as I was concerned, this app was a Big Deal.

The rating system later changed to a choice between a 5-star system, or a whopping 0–100 number system, 0 being "never play this again" and 100 being the best song the listener ever heard. The wide range of numbers and the ability to rate musical tastes so specifically allowed the algorithm to really shine. In other words, in all the time I used the app, as an avid song rater, it rarely played me a dud.

© Jess Stratton 2024
J. Stratton, *Copilot for Microsoft 365*, Inside Copilot,
https://doi.org/10.1007/979-8-8688-0447-2_1

In 2005, Pandora launched its consumer version of its similar music streaming service, the same one still used by about 50 million people today. While Pandora still currently allows users to rate a song using a thumbs-up or a thumbs-down system, its primary means of selecting songs based on users' preferences comes from the thousands of hours a handful of musicians and musicologists spent classifying songs at something called the Music Genome Project.

Founded in 2000 by Tim Westergren, the Music Genome Project's mission is to categorize music at its most fundamental levels based on over 450 "genetic" markers that combine to decode its root musical DNA. Using genetic terms is appropriate; after all, it's named after the more well-known Human Genome Project and functions in a similar manner. A collective group of musicians and musicologists have painstakingly cataloged over 60 years of music, spending upwards of 30 minutes on each song, carefully analyzing and categorizing markers such as harmonious melodies, vocal nuances in the singer's voice, whether the primary instrument is acoustic or electric, and even the amount of dissonance in a notable chord. (It was as recently as 2023 that Pandora finally updated the Music Genome Project to a tag-based system, making it easier for modern machine learning models to craft the listening experience.)

The Machines Learn How to Learn

Both LaunchCast and Pandora utilized a pre-artificial intelligence technique that hadn't yet had a name given to it. Today, we call it "supervised learning," a mechanism in which humans are directly responsible for teaching an algorithm how to choose its response in each situation. In LaunchCast, the humans were you, me, and anyone who used the service and rated the songs. In Pandora, the learning initially came from the musicians who cataloged the Music Genome Project and integrated that technology into the app. The *response* was the next song the apps would play.

While it wouldn't be until about 18 years later that "unsupervised learning" would come along, at least definitively titled as such, in the meantime, computers were being taught via programming how to search for patterns by themselves and choose how to respond. Today, chat AI technology has been pre-trained to create a predicted, generated response based on natural language: You enter your prompt in the chat window with what you're looking for, and the AI language model returns with text that is human-like in response.

When we think of machine learning algorithms, it's hard not to think of Facebook and the complex programming it takes to create an algorithm that lets a computer analyze our browsing habits and decide what it thinks we would like to see. However, even if you're not on social media, you've most likely been utilizing the services of an AI algorithm for a while – or at least come into some sort of relationship with it, voluntary or not. If you've ever used Gmail, it uses importance markers to decide what emails are important to you based on signals that include how often we communicate with that person, what specific words we use, and so on.

Google was also using AI in its infancy in the search bar. Aside from creating intelligence to determine common misspellings and instead search for the properly intended word or phrase, Google introduced an AI system called RankBrain in 2015. RankBrain's engine was designed to associate how words relate to concepts, and it used that knowledge to decide what order of importance to show you a site in its search results. This moment in time also marked the introduction of digital voice assistants like Apple's Siri, Amazon's Alexa devices, and Microsoft's Cortana, capable of interacting with you using natural language to perform basic tasks.

If YouTube has ever recommended a video to you or if you browse TikTok even remotely regularly, you've taken advantage of a machine-learned algorithm that has made a choice for you based on data from past or similar transactions. Spell check and autocorrect are all examples of programming that has been trained to anticipate what you're looking for to make your life easier, and that same autocorrect technology has been built with the assistance and reviews of linguists and computational analysts to create the algorithms. And, if you've ever cursed at a poorly phrased autocorrect, you've already learned that it's not perfect, doesn't always get it right, and absolutely needs monitoring for quality and accuracy. I'm sure you check your junk or spam filter for mail that inadvertently made its way in there incorrectly. Over time, you've no doubt learned, as I have, that monitoring, correcting, and adapting are all parts of the ways we use these tools. When you use AI to generate text, your responsibilities should be the same – monitoring, correcting, and adapting. If it sounds like a lot to worry about, don't worry – soon it will be a natural part of the way we all use the tool.

Even the customer service industry has been using something called *sentiment analysis* early on to detect the overall public opinion on a company's image. The collective posts from X (previously called tweets from Twitter) using a company's mentions or hashtags would be analyzed for words and phrases that indicated a customer had a positive opinion on the company *(great, fantastic, awesome)* versus negative words *(useless, poor, terrible, slow)*, indicating unhappiness and a negative opinion of the company.

As an avid tech trainer (and of course as a user), it's been amazing to watch the evolution of artificial intelligence to the benefit of us, the end users. Autocorrect once only changed words that *everyone* commonly misspelled. Now, as the computing, processing, and Internet speed of each personal device has grown, so has the sophistication. For example, autocorrect now also changes words that are meaningful to you, in addition to the collective masses, and can even change and adjust spelling and grammar for context *while you're still typing the sentence*. Incredible.

I can give you a very clear picture of how rapidly the artificial intelligence industry is evolving by summing it up in one sentence: ChatGPT, which is now a household name and has single handedly changed the way we work and think, was only launched in November of 2022. Sounds crazy, right? It's absolutely bonkers how quickly the technology has evolved and continues to evolve. Here's the thing: It's impossible to talk about any AI, Copilot included, without making sure you have a proper introduction to OpenAI.

OpenAI Is Created... and Begins Creating

While ChatGPT was launched to the masses in late 2022 and the AI technology would grow to be used by 180 million people as part of their daily lives, the product itself was developed by OpenAI, which was founded in 2015 as an artificial intelligence research organization. The founders list consisted of computer scientists and entrepreneurs, among them Trevor Blackwell, Greg Brockman, Ilya Sutskever, Andrej Karpathy, Vicki Cheung, Durk Kingma, Jessica Livingston, Pamela Vagata, John Schulman, Sam Altman, Elon Musk, and Wojciech Zaremba (Musk later left to focus on Tesla rather than continue a possible conflict of interest with OpenAI development).

In 2018, OpenAI released a report introducing the world to the concept of a "Generative Pre-trained Transformer" (that's where the GPT acronym comes from, most commonly associated with ChatGPT), a method of deep learning in which large language models (LLMs) are trained in an unsupervised manner to predict the next word in a sentence to generate text that *sounds* human.

Let's back up a bit.

Language Models Become... Larger

You'll hear the phrase *large language model* thrown around a lot when learning about generative AI. A large language model is an algorithm, a form of natural language processing that is based on probability and pattern recognition. In other words, the model is given partial sentences and is then taught how to predict via pattern matching, mathematics, and statistics what most likely should come next to complete the sentence.

Take this sentence for example:

I want to go to the _____.

There's plenty of words that *could* come next here, but there's also a definite set of words that could *not* go next, as it would cause the sentence to make no sense grammatically or practically. The words italicized below can't possibly work, so their candidacy as the next possible word can be eliminated.

I want to go to the _____.

store

car

museum

red

sad

jumping

Once the LLM has used this prediction method to construct the response, it's then taught to continuously transform itself, spreading into longer sentences, paragraphs, and continuing the response to even greater lengths. Given the large scope of the model's ability to predict, transform, summarize, and continuously generate content along with the vast bank of data it's been trained on, it's appropriately titled as a *large* language model.

What are those datasets the large language models are pre-trained on? Content, lots of content, most of which is found on the Internet: web pages, books, articles, journals, etc. Due to the nature of having to pre-train these language models, the various versions of ChatGPT are limited to answers that were acquired during the respective training scope of that particular version. For example, earlier versions of ChatGPT were limited to a result set dating September 2021 and before. In other words, previously if you had asked ChatGPT what movies a particular actor or actress has been in, it would have only returned those movies before September 2021, even if they've been in movies since then.

This very important backstory does have a purpose, I promise. It all comes back to why you're here, and that's to learn how to use Copilot. And again, it all comes back to OpenAI. Microsoft invested 1 billion toward OpenAI in 2019 and then an additional 10 billion in 2023. A large majority of these funds went toward computing power – the dominant currency in AI. Regardless, the investment opened the doors to integrating AI into Bing in the Microsoft Edge browser based on ChatGPT's technology. Then called Bing Chat (now simply called Copilot), users could harness the power of chat AI right in the browser itself, asking questions about content on any web page. While not an issue anymore, at the time, this was able to eliminate that pesky 2021 date scope barrier.

You may have previously used ChatGPT before or tried it in some way or situation. You may never have typed anything into an AI chat window before, or even *seen* one. Either scenario is perfectly fine for this book – I'm happy you're here, and even if you've chatted with AI before, it's always worth it to have at least a little refresher before we move onto using these scenarios in the Microsoft apps with Copilot, and this foundation can help you make better prompts – or, at the very least, gain an appreciation for the incredible amount of computation that occurs to make a machine sound human.

In fact, even though I started this book's history lesson starting at 1999 with a music streaming service, if you wanted to know when the *first* attempt at conversational AI was pioneered, we would need to go even further back to 1966 when a computer scientist at MIT named Joseph Weizenbaum created the first chatbot named ELIZA. The most popular use of ELIZA was taking the user through a back-and-forth conversation like the way a psychiatrist might interact with a patient, the user being the patient. While ELIZA was preprogrammed with canned responses and was not sophisticated enough to be used as a real tool, its primary purpose was to explore how we as humans interact with machines using natural language. ELIZA was, however, sophisticated enough to be capable of attempting the Turing test, Alan Turing's methodology that we still use to this day to determine whether a machine or computer system is impersonating a human being or not. (Fun fact: As recent as October 2023, ELIZA beat ChatGPT-3.5 in a Turing test performed by a UC San Diego study on artificial intelligence.)

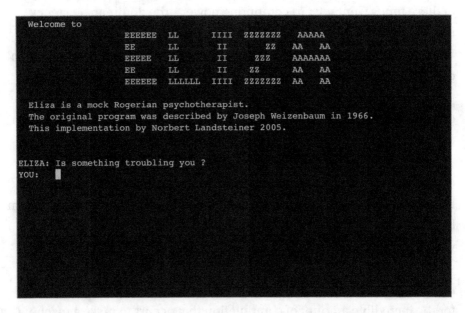

Figure 1-1. ELIZA is still available in its original form online through emulators

Another notable AI supercomputer capable of chatting in natural language is IBM Watson. Watson was developed to be a question-answering natural language system and made its debut in 2011 competing against humans on the television show *Jeopardy!*. Watson famously beat former champions Ken Jennings and Brad Rutter in one such match. Its winnings were donated to charity, and the world was given its first glimpse how a natural language chatbot can serve a *real* purpose – solving problems, sharing knowledge, and answering questions.

Chatting with a Machine Is Like Chatting with a Friend

Today's AI chat capabilities typically work in the same convenient, instant way you'd chat with a friend, or a customer service chat window. You can type your question into the chat window or ask the chat AI to generate something for you. All that computing power that previously examined the knowledge of those large datasets and transformed them into tokens that can recognize patterns then culminates into a response that sounds, seems, and feels like you're talking to another human being. And unlike a search engine, which starts over with a new search every time, you can continue your chat and retain the existing context of the conversation to refine the output with the chat AI, adding more context until you specifically start a new chat. You don't have to restate the problem every time; the context remains in that chat thread.

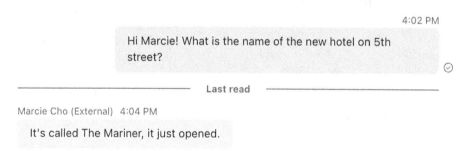

Figure 1-2. A sample conversion via Teams

Let's take the chat window from Microsoft Teams (as shown in Figure 1-2) as an example.

> Me: Hi Marcie! What is the name of the new hotel on 5th street?
>
> (Marcie Cho): It's called The Mariner, it just opened.

If I were to continue chatting, I could ask the following question:

> Me: Does it have a restaurant?

You'll notice I didn't need to restate any obvious information, such as the name of the place. Marcie knows that when I say *it*, I'm talking about that specific hotel.

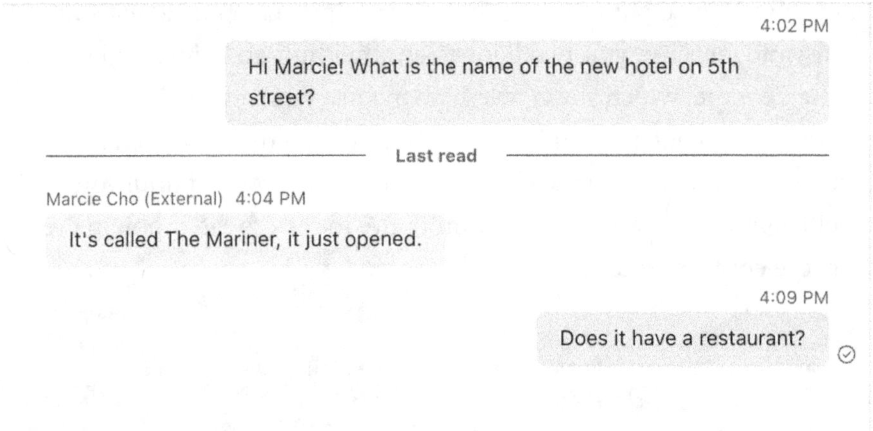

4:02 PM

Hi Marcie! What is the name of the new hotel on 5th street?

———————————————————— Last read ————————————————————

Marcie Cho (External) 4:04 PM

It's called The Mariner, it just opened.

4:09 PM

Does it have a restaurant?

Figure 1-3. *The word "it" tells Marcie I'm still talking about The Mariner restaurant*

Chatting with generative AI works the same way, and it's *almost* easy to forget that it's not an actual person chatting back at you.

Generative AI: The Basics

So with that, what kinds of things can you ask a generative AI model? It all starts with a prompt.

I could write an entire book on prompt engineering, and in fact, those do exist. At the end of this chapter, I'll cover a few of the technical names of the prompt techniques, but I'm more interested in making sure you know how to use the tools for maximum productivity. That's why you and I use the Microsoft apps every day – Word, Excel, Outlook, etc. – to get the most work done in the most efficient way. So, for that reason, I'll get you started with the basics.

Constructing a Prompt

What can you put into the prompt area/chat window? For the sake of the book, I'll be using terms like *chat window* and *prompt area*; those are the same thing.

If you've ever taken an online course by me or listened to me lecture, I'll always include my *golden rule*, and sure enough, any text you choose to put in your prompt follows the same principle: **There is no right or wrong way to create a prompt. Your prompts can be as simple or as complex as you need them to be to get the best possible results for what you're looking for.**

While the only *required* element is an actual request for something, a prompt can have a few key elements:

- An instruction-based request, whether it's a question or a request for content generation

- Context/framing guidelines to provide examples or provide background information that will make the response more specific to your needs

- Examples or a declaration of the specified desired output

Using Copilot in the Microsoft Edge browser, here's an example of a very basic prompt with a simple request, and only as much needed context as the request needs to be answered. Though not important, it's good to know this style of prompt is called a **direct** or **zero-shot** prompt.

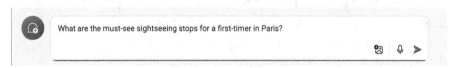

Figure 1-4. *A sample zero-shot prompt*

```
What are the must-see sightseeing stops for
a first-timer in Paris?
```

Here's another prompt, this time with some more context placed in the prompt itself.

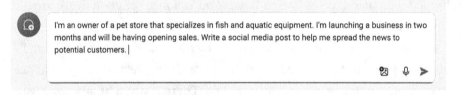

Figure 1-5. *A sample prompt containing a description of my business for additional context*

```
I'm an owner of a pet store that specializes
in fish and aquatic equipment. I'm launching
a business in two months and will be having
opening sales. Write a social media post
to help me spread the news to potential
customers.
```

Here's an example of the same scenario, except this time you can see the response from the previous request. I'll continue the prompt after a response is given, giving more context to refine the output.

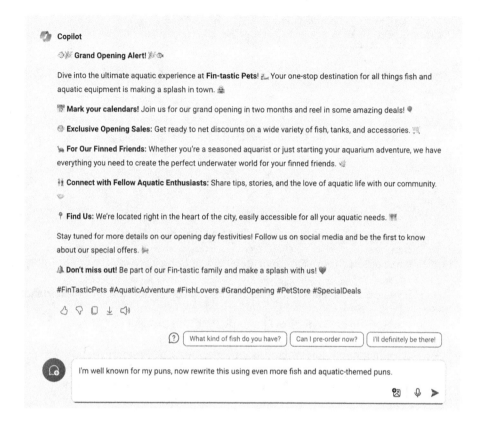

Figure 1-6. *The AI model has created a long social media post for me based on my context-filled request*

I won't keep you hanging, but you'd better believe that the output came through hook, line, and sinker (that pun was all me, no AI used there).

Here's an example of declaring a specific type of output for your prompt, assuming I'm still using the preceding examples as context.

Figure 1-7. *You can declare the specific type of output you are looking for*

```
Write five headlines for this in a
bulleted list.
```

Asking for output in that format will give me a nice, tidy list.

 You

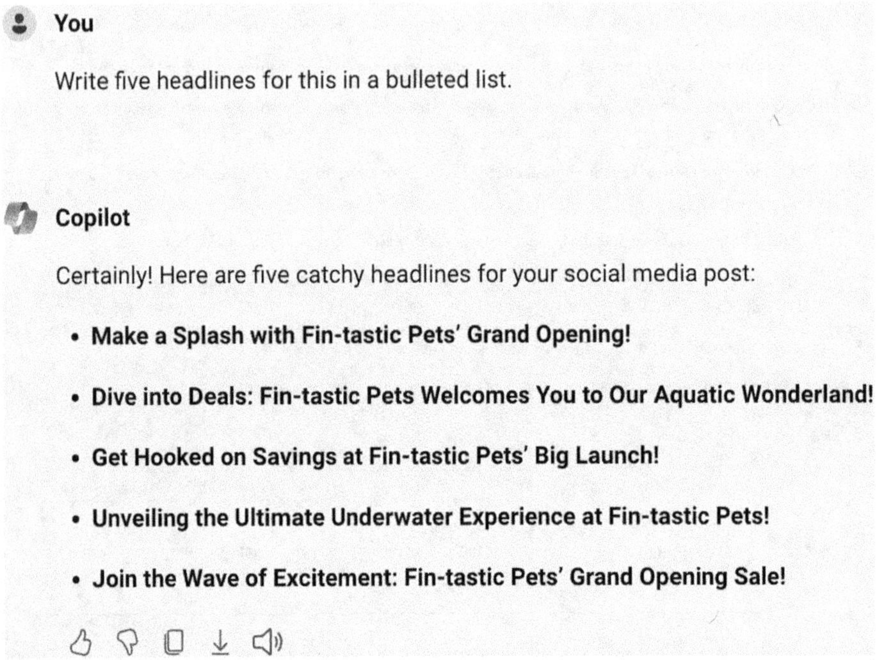

Write five headlines for this in a bulleted list.

 **Copilot**

Certainly! Here are five catchy headlines for your social media post:

- **Make a Splash with Fin-tastic Pets' Grand Opening!**

- **Dive into Deals: Fin-tastic Pets Welcomes You to Our Aquatic Wonderland!**

- **Get Hooked on Savings at Fin-tastic Pets' Big Launch!**

- **Unveiling the Ultimate Underwater Experience at Fin-tastic Pets!**

- **Join the Wave of Excitement: Fin-tastic Pets' Grand Opening Sale!**

👍 👎 🗐 ⬇ 🔊

Figure 1-8. *The output that the prompt yielded is in a bulleted list, just like I asked for*

Getting Different Types of Output

What types of ways can you get output from generative AI? Let me start by asking a different question: What's the most *effective* way for you to receive the data you requested from the AI?

You can get a summary. You can get bullet points. You can get a chart or a graph, and you can even have the response explained in a simpler language for you. You can get a numbered list, a poem, a song, a story, a blog post or social media post.

And with some versions of Copilot now including support for Dall-E, OpenAI's image generator, you can even create your own digital images. If a summary is too confusing or wordy, ask the AI to write it again in simpler language or make it shorter. If you're looking at a sea of words, try the same request, except this time ask for it in bullet points. If you didn't get enough ideas, ask for a few more.

```
Compare the top five small office printers
with pros, cons and price. Format the
results as a table.
```

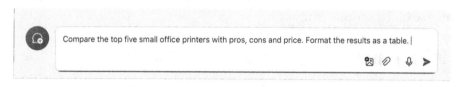

Figure 1-9. *I can specifically ask for the output as a table to make it easier for me to read*

```
Tell me how responsive web design works but
explain it like I'm five years old.
```

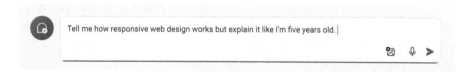

Figure 1-10. *A method of requesting the type of response I require. In this case, I'm asking for a simple explanation*

Before I end this chapter and move onto Copilot itself and how Microsoft 365 has evolved to get to the place where 345 million people rely on its cohesive apps to get their work done every day, here's a brief mini-glossary of some terms you'll come across in your journey to learn more about conversing with generative AI.

Large Language Model (LLM)

A large language model (LLM) is a deep learning algorithm of natural language processing that is based on probability and pattern recognition to generate phrases that sound human.

Generative Pre-trained Transformer (GPT)

Developed and named by OpenAI, a GPT is a model that is trained on a massive databank, which takes an input sequence called a token and, using mathematics and statistical probability, predicts the remaining phrase in the output sequence.

Hallucination

A hallucination is an incorrect, fabricated, or misleading response as output to a prompt that *sounds* correct. Hallucinations are usually due to an incorrect prediction or pattern of the LLM and GPT working together but can also be caused by incomplete training of the model, or training based on biased data. Most AI systems, including ChatGPT and Copilot, contain initial warnings that incorrect or factual errors can occur in the results of any prompt and that chatbots occasionally make mistakes. It's encouraged to always double-check responses, especially when financial, legal, or medical responses are involved or any request that relies on accurate information.

Zero-Shot (Direct) Prompting

Zero-shot (direct) prompting is the most basic and simplest prompt technique in which no examples or context is given in the initial prompt, just a request. The LLM will pull the predicted response only from the dataset it's been pre-trained on. *"What are some good indoor activities to do on a rainy day?", "Create a job description request for an entry-level marketing assistant."*

One-Shot and Few-Shot Prompting

One-shot prompting and few-shot prompting are two additional prompt methods, using one (one-shot) or multiple (few-shot) examples as context to guide and assist the response. *"Example: 'Like, OMG, I totes need a vacay like, now!.' Using the example, write a funny email requesting time off from work.", "Using data from Schematic.docx and Supplies.docx, write a non-technical summary of steps required to put the model together including what supplies are needed."*

Role-Based Prompting

Role-based prompting is a prompt technique in which you ask the AI system to take on a persona, thus controlling the tone, style, and content of the generated response. *"You are a customer service representative working at a health food company. Generate a response to a customer who is upset because they are not noticing any improvement in their symptoms after taking one of your most popular supplements."*

Chain of Thought Prompting

Chain of thought prompting is a prompt technique in which the prompt guides the model step by step through a request and asks for reasoning in the response. This method is useful for creative writing, essays, solving math problems, and using generative AI to assist with learning. *"Using data from EmployeeOnboarding.pptx, create three questions based on the slide deck. Make the questions multiple choice. Provide the reasoning for the correct answer."*

Prompt Engineering

Prompt engineering is a method of determining the best type of prompt to get the most useful response. As a large language model and GPT work together to predict the next words and phrases based on the context it's given, that context comes from the prompt that you'll create, and as you can see, there are many, many ways to create a prompt!

Intelligent User Interface

Intelligent user interface is an interface that a user can interact with that includes any type or variation of artificial intelligence. In the next chapter, I'll begin with a brief history of Microsoft's AI evolution, including the introduction of intelligent user interfaces. If you've been using Microsoft Office for many years, as I have, you no doubt will recognize the first example I list.

Summary

From streaming music services back at the turn of the century to OpenAI's ChatGPT, artificial intelligence has come a long way in a very short amount of time. Even if you don't use these services directly, you have most likely encountered a service-based artificial intelligence model, even if it's just chatting with a customer service agent online.

Today's generative AI models take your natural language input (called a *prompt*) and output a natural language response. You can change your prompt style to suit your needs (called *prompt engineering*), add more context, and continue the conversation. Up next, we'll talk about the history of artificial intelligence in Microsoft products.

CHAPTER 2

An Introduction to Microsoft Copilot

I started the book with a foundational history of chat AI because it makes it so much easier to segue into a discussion on how Copilot actually works, which in return will make it so much easier for you to learn it and maximize its benefits. Hopefully, you'll also even learn some new ways to use the apps that you may not already know about. As of this publication, there are now even multiple versions of Copilot for both enterprise and home users. While this book focuses on the enterprise version, I'll be going over the differences of each version in detail in Chapter 4. But long before Copilot arrived, Microsoft has been at the forefront of intelligent user interfaces created to assist its users.

The First Office Assistant Is Created – As an Animated Paperclip

While Microsoft Office itself was created in 1988, it was Office 97 that contained a few notable milestones in the annals of Office history. Released in late 1996, it was the first time the Office software suite contained a key code activation system as proof of purchase. It also introduced something called *command bars* – a unified system and look across each Microsoft Office app containing the toolbar and menu bar.

© Jess Stratton 2024
J. Stratton, *Copilot for Microsoft 365*, Inside Copilot,
https://doi.org/10.1007/979-8-8688-0447-2_2

And finally, it included a new intelligent user interface called the Office Assistant, which was included as part of the help files in Office 97. While Copilot today could certainly fall under the "Office Assistant" category, it is not the first assistant Microsoft has ever used, not by a longshot. No, back to the Office 97 debut, that honor would go to an animated paperclip first named Clippit and then later shortened to what it's now famously known as – Clippy.

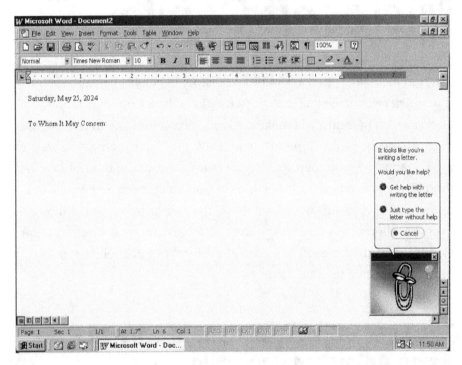

Figure 2-1. *Clippy in Office 97 appeared automatically as a response to various inputs in the document*

Clippy *tried* hard to be useful. It really did. I'm sure just by mentioning its name is bringing back memories for you if you've ever used it. While we were certainly emailing back then, letters were still the primary means of communication, and all it took was to open a new blank Word document, put the cursor on a new line, and type the word "Dear-" and Clippy dutifully, repeatedly offered to assist, even when we didn't need assistance. No one had time to learn how to disable Clippy, instead myself along with everyone else just made refusing its help a part of everyday office life. In fact, it made itself so much a part of our lives that Microsoft has immortalized Clippy in a series of sticker packs and emojis in Teams and Windows 11.

The Ribbon Arrives, As Does a Subscription Model

Clippy stuck around until Office 2007, another notable release from Microsoft as this is when the ribbon first made its introduction. Still in use today to ensure conformity, familiarity, and ease of use across the Microsoft suite, the ribbon is the tabbed interface at the top of apps like Word, PowerPoint, Excel, and Outlook. Each tab contains groups of commonly associated tasks, and some tabs are context-sensitive, meaning they only appear when certain objects are selected, or conditions are met.

While available as a private beta as early as 2010, it was in 2013 that Microsoft began offering its Microsoft Office suite of apps as a subscription with the introduction of Office 365, along with its first offering of a cloud-based version of the apps as well. From here, things escalate quickly. This is about the time when I started my online training career, teaching these apps with Lynda.com, now called LinkedIn Learning. It was not uncommon for me to have to re-record an entire course within the first few months of its release. For example, the cloud storage service SkyDrive, which had been a steadfast part of the Office suite since its introduction in 2007, got a user interface change to match Outlook.com in 2012. In 2013, SkyDrive would be renamed OneDrive, as it remains named to this day.

In 2020, Microsoft rebranded the consumer and small business versions of Office 365 to the more all-encompassing "Microsoft 365," and in 2022, Microsoft announced the Office brand would be phased out entirely, including the mobile suite of the apps and all enterprise versions.

The subscription-based version of these apps is an important step in the evolution of Copilot as it is today. While users can still buy the boxed desktop versions of Office 2013, 2016, and 2019 at a one-time purchase price, their license only allows for a fixed feature list that is included on the CD at the time of release and subsequent updates only include bug fixes and security patches. Subscribers who pay a monthly or yearly fee for Microsoft 365 can take advantage of frequent updates containing exciting new features and tools, many of which rely on an Internet connection to use and the enablement of something called Microsoft Intelligent Services.

Microsoft Puts Your Internet Connection to Work

Intelligent Services uses AI over the cloud to bring extra functionality to the Microsoft 365 apps. What does that mean? It means your data is temporarily sent over the Internet using your existing Internet connection over to Microsoft's servers, which then processes the request and sends the result back to you. Some tools are small and efficient, such as the **Tell Me** tool. Now just a search box at the top of the ribbon across the Microsoft apps, the box used to prompt the user with a friendly "Tell me what you want me to do..." cue in the search itself.

If you've never used it, it's wonderfully effective and takes a huge chunk of the learning curve out of the apps. You can simply type what you're looking for, whether it's the exact toolbar button ("Mail merge") or what you want to do but don't know what it's called. A choice of actions will be presented to you, which in many cases can be faster than clicking through ribbon tabs to find the same button.

Figure 2-2. *You can type what you're trying to do in the search bar*

Over time, Microsoft Intelligent Services has gotten even more intelligent and useful to save you time. You can use it to visually analyze your data in Excel, even if you're not adept at creating charts. You can slap an image and some text on a slide and use the Designer tool in PowerPoint to make it look professional. You can use a Quick Starter tool in PowerPoint to get a basic presentation started for you with just a few keywords. You can click a microphone icon in Word and dictate your document rather than typing it out, and the Immersive Reader feature can help you focus on what you're reading if you're easily distracted, need to change your reading experience, or are learning to read a language. In fact, Intelligent Services has been key in Microsoft's commitment to accessibility and inclusivity, both in using and creating documents. PowerPoint can even include live captions of your presentation if you have a microphone connected to your computer while you present, and a tool called Accessibility Checker in various apps can detect potential readability issues with your files and can help you make the suggested changes.

Due to the nature of your data being sent over the Internet and then returned to you, I did want to mention that users were always able to read Microsoft's privacy policy and opt out of using Intelligent Services in the Options screen of the app; however, these options have since been phased out in favor of more advanced privacy controls, some of which are administrator-controlled.

It's also important to note that these tools have never been phased out because of Copilot. They still exist, are regularly used, and are incredibly powerful, and I personally also rely on them to be more productive daily. I mention them as part of a history lesson because they are all part of the natural progression and software evolution to get to where we are now.

Microsoft Introduces Your New Copilot for Work

In spring of 2023, Microsoft announced a new evolution in productivity – Copilot – and later branched it out into different products. There's **Copilot for Microsoft 365** for enterprise users and **Copilot Pro** for home and family subscribers. There's also a free version simply called **Copilot** you can access on the web with limited functionality.

Copilot for Microsoft 365 and Copilot Pro introduce prompt chatting in the Microsoft apps themselves – Word, PowerPoint, Excel, Outlook, and other apps including Teams *(not available in Copilot Pro)*. While the initial version for the apps wouldn't be officially released and available until late September 2023, the announcement, along with the idea of using natural language chatting to get work done, took the world by storm.

This wasn't the first Copilot product; other products had been quietly introduced using that name, and I'll talk about them in the last chapter. What made the nature of *this* particular announcement so astounding was due to the integration of generative AI in not only our work data but also the Microsoft apps we use every day.

I talked about how you can already use OpenAI's ChatGPT to get questions answered, solve problems, and compose text. I also told you earlier how Microsoft integrated some of that technology in its Edge browser to use natural language to do things like summarize the contents of a long web article. As the majority of the Microsoft 365 apps are all fully functional on the web, Bing Chat (now simply Copilot) made it possible to summarize and generate content from Word documents, Excel, and Outlook emails as long as you were logged in and had the files open on the browser. Copilot for Microsoft 365 now takes it much further than that – allowing that same prompt technology into the desktop versions of the apps. This means that you can get context-related questions answered, ask for summaries, and generate text based on your everyday business-related files and documents.

This book is focused on the *enterprise* version of Copilot – Copilot for Microsoft 365. In Chapter 4, I'll discuss the various versions of Copilot, who the intended target audience is, and what each version costs, but the book is primarily focused on the benefit you'll gain in your workday using Copilot for Microsoft 365 to connect to your organization's tenant. It does this through something called the *Microsoft Graph*, and that's a programming model that's unique to Microsoft 365 and the enterprise security platform.

Figure 2-3. *Copilot's Graph-grounded chat, as seen when logged in with your work sign-in on microsoft365.com*

In short, it's a game-changer. Soon it won't be as necessary to remember how to use Word, or Excel, or how to create a presentation in PowerPoint; *it will only be necessary to know how to ask Copilot to perform the task for you.* It won't be as necessary to remember how to use functions in Excel, or even to stay as organized in Outlook. Copilot for Microsoft 365 can keep track of all that business data for you and display it to you as you need it and when you need it.

So, what exactly makes Copilot for Microsoft 365 so different from opening a browser and using ChatGPT, or even Copilot in a browser? The difference is the complex system of elements that all work together to make it safe and effective to use chat AI with your precious business data. Let's examine all the parts about Copilot for Microsoft 365, including Microsoft Graph-grounded chat – asking general research questions from the web but *also* questions about your organization's internal chats, emails, files, meetings, and people.

Remember, you won't be able to do this with Copilot Pro, the home or family version (to be discussed in Chapter 4), nor can you do this with Copilot's web-grounded chat. It's strictly a benefit that Copilot for Microsoft 365 enterprise users will enjoy.

The Elements That Make Up Copilot

Remember those LLMs, also known as large language models? I mentioned earlier that you'd hear that terminology a lot, and Copilot is no exception. Integrating the power of generative AI into your everyday business data requires a few key elements, all working together. These aren't things you need to acquire before you can use it; it's just a discussion of how all these elements are coordinated, making it all work. It all starts with the LLMs.

Large Language Models

The different versions of Copilot use a few LLMs. One of those is a version of OpenAI's ChatGPT-4. The free Copilot and Copilot Pro use DALL-E 3's image AI large language model, also by OpenAI, which makes it possible to create and analyze images. It's interesting that Copilot for Microsoft 365 *cannot* use DALL-E 3 to create and analyze images in the apps themselves, but you can do that with Copilot's web-grounded chat. I'll be showing you how to switch to web-grounded chat with commercial data protection to accomplish this in Chapter 10, so don't worry – you aren't missing out on anything!

These large language models used by Copilot are hosted in the Microsoft Cloud, specifically the Azure OpenAI service. Here's one thing that sets Copilot apart: The fact that it's hosted on Microsoft's servers means that it's not using the same chat engine that's powering OpenAI's ChatGPT-4 that the general public uses – it's all Microsoft. OpenAI does not have access to Copilot's language models or data that goes through them.

Commercial Data Protection

Here's another benefit that Copilot for Microsoft 365 users receive from Microsoft: commercial data protection, at no additional cost. Copilot for Microsoft 365 is *never* trained on your business private data, and it won't be trained on any new knowledge it gains while you chat. Your prompts and Copilot's responses are not retained.

Formerly called Bing Chat Enterprise, Copilot with commercial data protection checks to make sure you're logged in with your Microsoft Entra ID, which is just a fancy way of saying your work ID. The sign-in verification is so Copilot knows to give you this protection for your web-grounded chats. You won't see the protected symbol when you're using Graph-grounded chat.

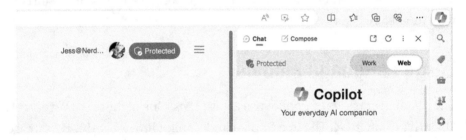

Figure 2-4. *The Protected icon is there so you'll know you're logged in and using Copilot with commercial data protection*

Wait a minute – I 've been using that phrase quite a bit. What is Graph-grounded chat? And if Copilot isn't trained on your company data, how is it possible to get questions answered and content generated about it? How can it know about data it's not trained on? Before we can talk about Graph-grounded chat, we need to talk about the next component, the Microsoft Graph.

Microsoft Graph

The Microsoft Graph is a single, unified element in your organization that contains access to your core business data stored on Microsoft 365. What kind of data? Your emails, meetings and calendar events, contacts, tasks, Teams chats, files stored on OneDrive, SharePoint, Bookings, notes created on OneNote, and other Microsoft apps. The Microsoft Graph existed before Copilot did. It was created so developers didn't have to have a separate application programmer interface (API) for each element of Microsoft they needed to access to create their own tools for their organizations.

Let's take this situation before the Graph existed: A developer is creating an interface or a tool that asks the user for a specific date, which will then display a list of emails received and calendar events occurring on that date. To accomplish this, the developer is required to have and use several different groups of code. These groups of code, called application programmer interfaces, or APIs, contain the special programming functions that each module needs. To access the individual areas of the required Microsoft apps, the developer will need the API for Outlook email, and the API that Teams requires, and oh, of course, the Outlook calendar has its own API calls, so they'll need that one as well.

The Microsoft Graph was created to bring all these APIs together. Now, the developer only needs access to the Microsoft Graph API, and with it comes the ability to access the data in each aspect of the Microsoft apps the developer needs. In Copilot for Microsoft 365, the Microsoft Graph is how it gains the required context of your business to create responses to your prompts.

It can access the contents of your Word documents, your Outlook email, your contacts, and the people in your organization. When you ask Copilot to summarize an email or analyze a column of Excel data, it's using the Microsoft Graph to access the code required to gain access to that data.

I realize and understand that this is *far* more technical an explanation than you need, but so many of these elements are going to be more and more prevalent in future revisions and technologies. You'll be able to pick up what's going on far more quickly with this foundation and read and understand technical articles much more clearly.

Not only have I used the term *Graph-grounded chat*, I've also mentioned that there's a *web-grounded chat*. Let's back up a bit again to talk about the next component, grounding, and what it means.

Grounding

In the artificial intelligence world, grounding is a *process*. Behind the scenes, it's how the model connects abstract knowledge, symbolic representations, and natural language into trusted sources of information or specific data, context, or examples.

Copilot with Microsoft Graph-Grounded Chat

When you use Copilot and your prompts are Microsoft Graph-grounded, it means that the LLM can use context and information from Microsoft Graph, which as you now know is data specific to your work or organization. This makes responses relevant and accurate enough to perform tasks like generating content based on your files, catching up on meetings you missed, and getting the most up-to-date answers to questions based on your work data.

I have chapters on using Copilot in Word, Excel, PowerPoint, Outlook, and Teams. Copilot in the Microsoft 365 apps is used in a very specific way. You can generate content for use in those apps, you can ask questions about the current file or meeting that you're working on, and you can ask for assistance accomplishing tasks in those apps.

Chapter 10, however, is a little different. It's specifically on Copilot with Microsoft Graph-grounded chat. This is a special chat you can have with Copilot in which you can ask all sorts of questions about your organization. In fact, you can ask about any of those items I mentioned that the Microsoft Graph covers – your schedule, someone else's schedule that you're allowed to access, emails, documents, etc.

Copilot with Web-Grounded Chat

So, now we know that Copilot will look to the Microsoft Graph for additional context and relevant information to ground against enterprise data. If that's true, then what happens when you're looking for information that's *not* work related, or outside the organization? This time, Copilot will use *web grounding*, meaning it will use context and information from the Internet, specifically Bing search instead of the Microsoft Graph.

When you access Copilot for Microsoft 365 on the web (and I'll show you how to do that in Chapter 10), you can switch between Microsoft Graph-grounded chat and web-grounded chat with commercial data protection.

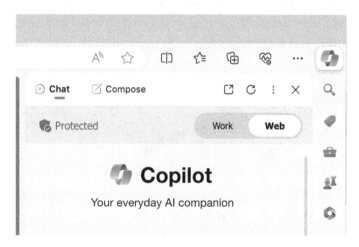

Figure 2-5. *The toggle switch to change between Microsoft Graph-grounded chat and web-grounded chat is in the Edge sidebar and at* `https://copilot.microsoft.com`

The grounding process is there to make sure your results are accurate and relevant. You may be worried about letting loose a process that can gather information from your data for someone else in your organization. Please don't be – Copilot's responses to you *only* contain the data that you should know about and are allowed to pull from. Copilot can only access data that you have access to. It uses existing Microsoft 365 role-based access controls.

When you prompt Copilot for a response and it goes searching the Microsoft Graph for relevant data, it knows that there are policies and security permissions already in place and it respects those. The search is performed in context as *you*, meaning it's only going to search and return data you already have access to.

The search against the data in the Microsoft Graph is always prioritizing relevant content, and it does that via multiple signals including keywords, personalization, and social matching, which is you and the closeness of your work network and teammates.

Copilot for Microsoft 365 takes this one step further by adding a *conceptual understanding* of the data you have access to in order to better understand the intent of your query, which leads to more relevant responses. It does this through something called the semantic index.

The Semantic Index

The semantic index enhances the existing Microsoft 365 search by using something called *semantic search*. Semantic search uses vectored indices. It's important to note that a lot of these search options can be overridden by any role-based search or indexing parameters set by your organization administrator. These are things you can't change; remember, this isn't a book for *administering* Copilot or Microsoft 365, it's a book for reaping the benefits of it.

Speaking of reaping the benefits, it's time for the last element of Copilot, and the one that matters to you the most – the apps and the chat prompts themselves!

The Microsoft 365 Apps and Microsoft Graph-Grounded Chat

Where will you be using Copilot for Microsoft 365? In the desktop apps themselves, online at microsoft365.com, or the **Work** tab at copilot. microsoft.com.

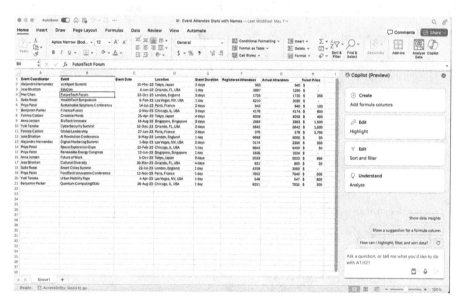

Figure 2-6. *In the desktop apps, such as Excel shown here, Copilot appears as a sidebar item*

When you use Copilot in the Microsoft 365 apps themselves (Word, PowerPoint, Excel, etc.), you'll be using it to help you use those apps better, or create or analyze content within that app. When you use it online or in Microsoft Teams, you'll be using Copilot with Microsoft Graph-grounded chat. This allows you to chat with Copilot about your work data. Don't worry about that for now – I have chapters on each of these apps and Microsoft 365 with Graph-grounded chat to give you specific ways you can use Copilot to help you.

What, Specifically, Can You Do with Copilot?

Knowing what you now know – the width and breadth of the power of Copilot across Microsoft 365, the only hard part now is coming to terms with the large amounts of problems that Copilot can solve for you. I'll show you more examples in the later chapters, but here are some ideas to get you started:

> *Based on emails from the past month, is my client happy with the progress we are making with the San Francisco hotel expansion project?*

> *Are any of my team members out of the office next week?*

> *How can I talk to a coworker who is taking my lunch out of the fridge?*

> *Give me 20 titles for a new podcast about managing large projects.*

> *Create a PowerPoint presentation based on the data and charts from YearlyProjections.xlsx.*

> *Create a social media post suitable for LinkedIn based on this document.*

> *Summarize what I missed in the meeting from the last 30 minutes.*

I've mentioned a few times about responsible AI – up next, I'll give you a brief overview of AI ethics. It's not a deep dive – that's not what this book is about. There's plenty of information about that, but you do need to have at least a basic understanding of how it works, what responsible AI development is, and how it affects *your* use of artificial intelligence to create content and use the results.

Summary

Microsoft has been using foundational artificial intelligence in its suite of Office apps since 1996, starting with the personal assistant "Clippit," a.k.a. "Clippy," an animated paperclip that assisted users with various tasks. Since then, Microsoft Intelligent Services has been adding features utilizing AI throughout Microsoft 365 releases, such as analyzing data in Excel or redesigning slides in PowerPoint.

Announced in 2023 as Copilot and now formally known as Copilot for Microsoft 365, the ability to use chat technology within the Microsoft apps excited the world. Along with generating content and asking questions about the current file in the apps themselves, Copilot for Microsoft 365 comes with Microsoft Graph-grounded chat. Discussed in detail in Chapter 10, this is the same prompt-based chat you're familiar with, except grounded in the context of Microsoft Graph. That is, you have the ability to ask questions all about your work data – emails, meetings, people, files, and schedules.

CHAPTER 3

A (Brief) Introduction to Responsible AI

Just to get this out of the way first, this is a book on how to use AI as a tool to help you in your daily work life within the Microsoft 365 environment. It's *not* a book on AI ethics. Such books exist, but amidst such a rapidly emerging environment, I'm sure they need to be updated on an almost daily basis. I welcome you to do your own exploring online at the vast legislature that's both been passed and in progress. You can read about the EU Artificial Intelligence Act (what is shaping to be the first multinational legislation around AI) and what the United States is thinking about on a federal level targeting AI law versus what legislature individual states have already passed. In fact, if you look up AI regulations in the country you're in, there's probably a few plans in the works to govern artificial intelligence.

That said, you may have concerns, and if so, you're absolutely, positively 100% not alone in that regard. Fear of "the machines," robots, and artificial intelligence taking over your job, visions of the future from the movie *Terminator 2*, there's probably not a soul out there who hasn't had at least a fleeting worry about these things.

There are two reasons I spent the first two chapters explaining the behind-the-curtain workings of both Copilot and generative AI. The first is so that you'll have a more solid grasp and appreciation of the programming and algorithms and at least some of the pieces of what goes into making text sound like it's coming from a human.

© Jess Stratton 2024
J. Stratton, *Copilot for Microsoft 365*, Inside Copilot,
https://doi.org/10.1007/979-8-8688-0447-2_3

The second reason is more important. Hopefully, it's helped demystify the process for you and will help make your AI experience just a bit smaller and less overwhelming and possibly alleviate any fears of the robots taking over, at least imminently. If you still aren't sold yet, remember how much time, effort, and programming went into developing the AI systems in the first place? What if I told you that just as much time, effort, and programming has equally gone into making sure this technology is being created responsibly?

Wait, let's back up again. What does that even mean?

Responsible AI Development

Let's start by making sure we're all on the same page as to what developing and creating artificial intelligence *responsibly* means. It's such a fast-growing technology in both creation and widespread use that the need for safeguards is imperative.

Responsible AI entails considering both ethics and legality during the creation, deployment, and use of artificial intelligence.

Every software company that creates and deploys artificial intelligence should have a responsible AI policy, that is, an approach and declaration of the care and caution they plan on taking when developing their apps. In other words, an assurance that they have prioritized safety and ethics, and that we can stand by their trustworthiness.

While there are some basic frameworks that companies can use to create their set of standards, there's no one-policy-fits-all solution, so it is important to note that at the end of the day, it's up to each company to make sure they are being transparent and safe to earn that level of trustworthiness.

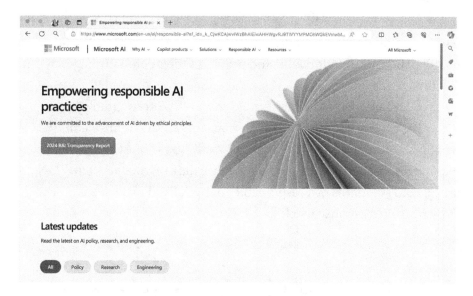

Figure 3-1. *Microsoft's website on responsible AI*

Safety Considerations in AI

Just like in real life, safety in AI has multiple meanings and layers. There's the most obvious layer – an AI system should never result in damage to property or the environment. It should never result in human harm. It should also never result in discrimination or prejudice, which can occur as a result of a biased training system.

And finally, besides the physical layers, an AI system should also be secure and protected against attacks such as hackers.

Determining an AI's Trustworthiness

Aside from making sure the company has provided a responsible AI policy, you can also look for transparency in the company's disclosure of the product. For example, while I'll get to Microsoft's responsible AI practices in a moment, I've already completely covered how Copilot works from the backend. That wasn't supersecret information I was privy to. No, Microsoft has all of this information loud and proud on their company pages about Copilot.

In addition, many AI systems hold themselves accountable by including a feedback mechanism for inaccurate, bad, or misleading responses directly next to the response itself. Some, like Copilot, even include direct citations where the response data originated from. These are all gold standards of a responsible AI model and make it easy for you to fact-check the response itself.

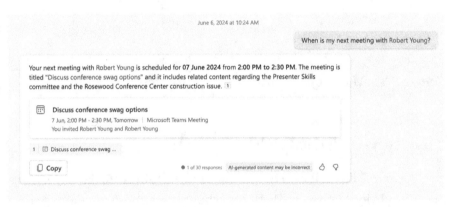

Figure 3-2. *Copilot has explained the answer, provided a reference citation with a link, and given a thumbs-up/down mechanism for reporting the quality of the response*

I mentioned in the glossary at the end of Chapter 1 that one type of prompt technique involves directly asking the AI model to explain how it arrived at its response. That explanation is an indirect way to look at the transparency of the model itself and can even be used as a quick method of fact-checking the system.

The Risks of Using Generative AI

In 2009, a young gentleman named Desi Cryer became a viral YouTube sensation when he demonstrated some technology in his new laptop with his coworker, Wanda. His HP MediaSmart laptop had recently introduced facial-tracking software into its webcam software. Innovative for its time, the software allowed the app to track movement when a person used the camera. The video, famously titled "HP computers are racist," contained a laughing but puzzled Desi and his coworker as they demonstrated that the camera did not detect Desi, who is Black, but immediately detected and correctly followed Wanda, his white coworker. While the video was created all in good fun and Desi and Wanda never intended their case to become a viral discussion on race and ethics, HP's response was swift. While they did acknowledge the shortcoming, they explained the technology had difficulty seeing contrast when there was insufficient foreground lighting.

A Biased Dataset Can Lead to Biased Responses

The preceding HP example, while obviously not a generative AI system, still clearly illustrates that algorithms that learn on biased datasets can and will yield biased results. In HP's example, the facial detection clearly was optimized for better contrast against lighter skin. Not only that, the quality control and testing group did not seem to include enough people of color, or the issue would have been discovered and fixed far before being released to the general public.

A large language model is just as susceptible to these types of biases while it's being trained on each dataset. If that dataset contains biased data, so will the model. I'm not trying to paint a bleak outlook on all responses you will get from using any generative AI tool, including Copilot, but it's a risk you and anyone who uses AI tools need to be aware of. In the case of ChatGPT, OpenAI has made it very clear in the name of responsible AI and transparency that there is a need to critically assess responses that could potentially reinforce stereotypes and biases.

41

Even Microsoft was not immune to early blunders and errors in judgement in the name of innovation. In 2016, it created an AI Twitter chatbot named "Tay" that was created to be an experiment in "conversational understanding." Tay was programmed to adapt to conversation the more other Twitter users chatted with and engaged Tay in conversation. It took a mere 16 hours for Tay to be shut down due to the inappropriate responses it was coming up with. As Tay could learn from its interaction with other people, Tay could be manipulated into responding to even innocent conversations with abhorrent, vile tweets that were racist and vulgar in nature. In short, Twitter showed Tay what the worst of humanity could be.

In 2014, Amazon had been steadily creating its own AI recruiting tool that scanned resumes to quickly be able to recognize top talent and deployed the tool in 2015. It did not take long for Amazon to realize that its shiny new system had a strong bias against women. It took even less time to realize that a system scanning resumes from the past 10 years in a male-dominated industry at the time would lead to an AI system that penalized the word "women" and made it difficult to bring those resumes to the list of top talent.

While striving to achieve some transparency of my own in this book, I felt it necessary to include such examples, even as I'm reminded of what an icky time that was. However, I'm an optimist, and while this chapter and these anecdotes are necessary to teach you the very real risks of using AI, at the end of the day, it's a tool like any other. And when it's used the way it was meant to be used, it will help your business communication, speed up your research projects, and help keep you on track with your projects.

Garbage in means garbage out, and these early innovations and failures were critical and necessary to illustrate the need for responsible AI. The true takeaway, and the shining beacon of hope I want you to get from these stories, is that the very companies that had those early innovations and blunders are the very companies that learned from them and are the ones blazing the trail of what responsible AI means.

An AI Response Can Be Very Wrong, but Sound Very Correct

Michael Crichton is one of my absolute favorite authors. His writing is superb and immersive, and when I found myself reading his scientific explanations on quantum technology in his book *Timeline*, I remember thinking to myself, "that sounds so real and well-explained, why *can't* we do this now?" Obviously, we cannot because he was a science fiction writer, emphasis on the *fiction*, but I'm using this example of a different kind of risk when using generative AI.

As I discussed in the glossary at the end of Chapter 1, a hallucination is a term for an incorrect, fabricated, or misleading response as output to a prompt that *sounds* correct. Sometimes it's obvious, such as when you ask an image to be identified that's very clearly a flower vase, and the response tells you it's an elephant. But, sometimes, just like the late, great Michael Crichton, it gives a response that sounds so plausible, so factual, so *correct*, you'd be hard-pressed to even think twice about doubting it. And yet that answer is so, so wrong.

I'll talk in a moment about what you can do to help mitigate some of these risks, but the immediate answer here would be to make sure you're fact-checking as you go. You can do this yourself, or you can also follow up the response by asking the AI to explain its reasoning as to how it arrived at that answer.

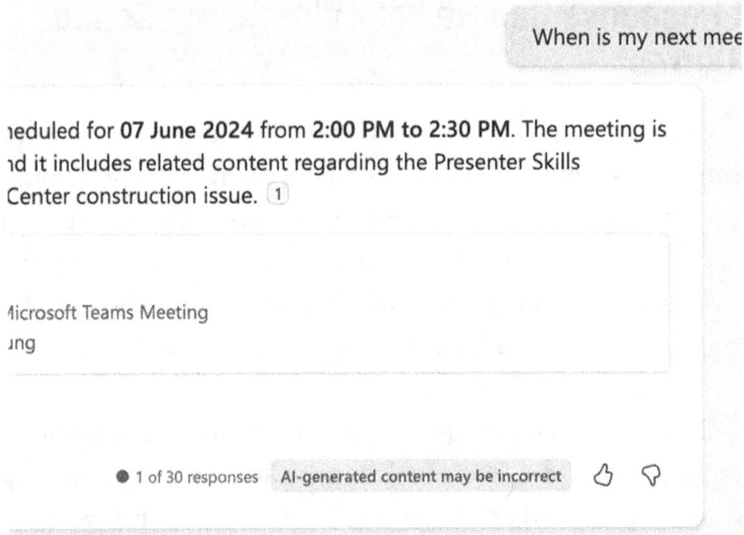

When is my next mee

ieduled for **07 June 2024** from **2:00 PM to 2:30 PM**. The meeting is
id it includes related content regarding the Presenter Skills
Center construction issue. ①

licrosoft Teams Meeting
ing

● 1 of 30 responses   AI-generated content may be incorrect   👍 👎

Figure 3-3. *Note the disclaimer: "AI-generated content may be incorrect"*

Authors and Artists Are Upset Their Works Are Being Used to Train AI

It's possible to ask generative AI to create a work in the style of a famous
author, such as Dr. Suess. While he's not alive to be upset about his style's
likeness being used to create brand-new works, thousands of other authors
are upset about large language models being trained on their hard-worked
skill so that others can create works that sound like them. In addition,
artists are also aware that their unique styles and talents are being used to
train AI models that can draw and create just like them as well.

Authors and artists are understandably upset as AI machines are being
trained on their writings and their style and AI image generators are being
used to create book covers instead of illustrators.

More and more companies are creating their own internal policies about where AI can be used, what it can be used for, and where they publish it. For example, a company may have a policy in place where generative AI can be used for research purposes but cannot be used when the response content is published elsewhere, for example, specifically generated for use in social media or blogs.

Microsoft's Commitment to Responsible AI

Like OpenAI, Google, and Adobe, Microsoft has a website dedicated to viewing their responsible AI commitments and policies. They are guided by six principles that define their development and use of AI:

- Fairness
- Reliability and safety
- Privacy and security
- Inclusiveness
- Transparency
- Accountability

In a publicly viewable document titled Microsoft Responsible AI Standard, v2 (June 2022), Microsoft lists their standards for individual goals, scenarios, and assessment criteria in its AI development and use. For example, there is an assessment to see if a particular AI system (such as Copilot) meets any definitions of restricted or sensitive use, and if so, to report them to the Office of Responsible AI to address any additional requirements and check against oversight for any possible adverse impact to the people that will use the system.

Another standard is their goal of disclosing when a person could be interacting with AI when it's not so obvious, for example, an AI system that generates images, art, and video.

How Does a Document of Guidelines Turn into Real-World Practices?

Let's take creating images with Copilot as an example. I mentioned earlier that Microsoft has partnered with DALL-E 3 to include image generation in the free Copilot with web grounding. I'll be going over some uses when you might want or need to create an image, but the important fact here is that the image has been solely created by AI, not a human. Microsoft has some responsible AI safeguards in place to honor their commitment I mentioned earlier. For starters, the AI will not generate harmful images, such as one containing nudity or violence. When a potentially hazardous image is detected, it will be blocked and a notification sent.

Originally, the AI model also blocked image creation of an artist, celebrity, or brand. Microsoft has since allowed this but has put in place a request form if the artist, celebrity, or brand in question wants to limit or stop it from happening. To give you more of an idea how much this is a constantly changing and evolving landscape, this ruling has happened in between me starting this book and making it only to Chapter 3 and typing this sentence!

In addition, any images that Copilot creates will have an invisible watermark on it. Microsoft has implemented special metadata attached to all its generated images called **Content Credentials**. This means that the image will be labeled as being created by AI with the time and date of its creation, a standard created by the *Coalition for Content Provenance and Authenticity*, otherwise known as C2PA. This watermark can be seen when the image is shared through a browser.

You can view Microsoft's responsible AI practices here: www.microsoft.com/en-us/ai/responsible-ai.

Your Role in Mitigating the Risks of Generative AI

A product such as Copilot for Microsoft 365 is meant to be used to help make you productive and efficient. This can help you get more time back, and it also has the potential to affect your organization's bottom line. These reasons alone are worth the use of the product, but like the Spider-Man franchise's most famous quote, "with great power comes great responsibility."

See if your company already has an AI acceptable use policy. Learn what your employer says you can use generative AI for with work projects and when or where you absolutely cannot. If you use a new generative AI product or app, look for the developer's list of responsible AI principles.

Humanize the responses you read. Is there anything immediately off about it? Can you follow the cited links and check the sources? Does it contain any harmful language? You can and should always use the feedback buttons to share poor responses.

Don't use personal or sensitive data in the prompt box. You should expect that a real human eye will be going over prompt data, both for quality control and for future development. The exception to this rule is when using Copilot for Microsoft 365 in an enterprise environment, in which you can expect corporate security and privacy to be honored, but otherwise, leave the nuclear codes and social security numbers out of your prompts.

Treat generative AI as first-draft quality. Don't copy and paste the output. Instead, use it as a guide to get you started. Expand on it, build from it, change it, and make it yours. If there is a time or a need to use AI output verbatim, consider disclosing that the text was created by AI.

47

Summary

Responsible AI entails considering both ethics and legality during the creation, deployment, and use of artificial intelligence. Artificial intelligence has had early failures from companies who did not yet realize the potential for bias in their products. These companies have since learned the importance of responsible AI policies and make them visible and transparent for both employees and end users to follow and read.

There are still risks involved when using generative AI products. Those risks include biased, incorrect, or harmful responses. You can help mitigate these risks by using the designated feedback mechanisms, seeing if your company has an acceptable use policy for generative AI, and treating responses as first draft only.

CHAPTER 4

Accessing Copilot

Before I can show you the fun of using Copilot, I first must make sure you can access Copilot. The waters are murky; it's extremely unglamorous to sort and filter the ever-changing information on web pages, news releases, and articles. Not to worry – I've done the work for you here and the information is current as of this publishing. Let's dive right in!

There are three main branches of Copilot, that is, ways you can access and use it:

- You can use Copilot on the web in a limited fashion with a free Microsoft account. This product is simply called **Copilot**.

- You can purchase Copilot as an add-on with your personal or family Microsoft 365 subscription to use it on the web *and* in your desktop apps. This product is called **Copilot Pro**.

- You or your employer can purchase Copilot as an add-on with your business or enterprise Microsoft 365 subscription to use it on the web *and* in your desktop apps. This is called **Copilot for Microsoft 365**, and it's the main product I'm focusing on in this book.

To help demystify these different variations of Copilot, I'm going to talk about all three of these branches along with the cost and requirements of each.

© Jess Stratton 2024
J. Stratton, *Copilot for Microsoft 365*, Inside Copilot,
https://doi.org/10.1007/979-8-8688-0447-2_4

Copilot – For Consumers with a Free Microsoft Account

If you have a free Microsoft account, you can enjoy the use of Copilot absolutely free, from a browser or mobile app. This means you don't need a Microsoft 365 subscription at all to take advantage of Copilot, in a limited fashion at least. This product is simply called **Copilot**.

You can sign up for a free Microsoft account at https://account. microsoft.com. Even if you have no Microsoft account, you'll click **Sign in** here.

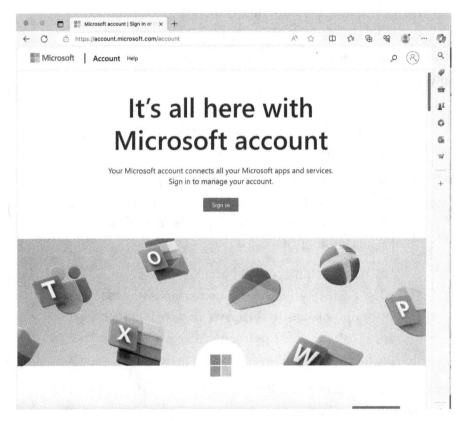

Figure 4-1. *The sign-in screen to create a new Microsoft account. Even if you have no account, choose "Sign in" here*

You'll be brought to a screen where you can either enter your existing Microsoft account sign-in or click the link to create one for free.

Figure 4-2. *Click the "Create one!" hyperlink if you don't already have a Microsoft account*

Once you have that Microsoft account (or existing Hotmail/Outlook. com/msn.com/live.com/Xbox Live account) you can access Copilot on the web at `https://copilot.microsoft.com`. I'll be giving you some examples on how you can use this free version to enjoy Copilot with web-grounded chat in Chapter 10, so for now, this is all about just getting access. You can use Copilot with web-grounded chat on Windows or MacOS or download the app on the Google Play store for Android or App store for iPad/iPhone.

Limitations of the Free Copilot

With this free version, you'll be able to take advantage of access to the better performing and more accurate GPT-4 only during nonpeak times for your prompts (during peak times, you'll be limited to GPT-3.5 while the large language model prioritizes its computation power for paying customers).

The free Copilot does *not* come with commercial data protection. That means that while using web-grounded chat, you won't see the protected logo I showed you in Chapter 2. Your prompts and corresponding responses from Copilot will be used to train the large language models.

In addition, with a free Microsoft account, you can also use Designer (formerly called Bing Image Creator) to create your own AI images but with some limitations. For example, in Designer, you'll only get 15 daily boosts for those images.

Wait – What the Heck Is a Boost?

A boost is *not* the number of images you can create in a day, though it certainly sounds like it should be. Rather, a boost is a single-use token that gives you faster processing time to get your image created. I'm sure by now you're really starting to understand how processing power truly is the currency of AI.

If you run out of tokens by creating or revising a created image, you can absolutely continue to work; however, your image prompts will get much lower priority and your image will take longer to render and appear for you.

Copilot Pro – For Consumers with a Personal or Family Microsoft 365 Account

This section is for consumers that have purchased an existing personal or family Microsoft 365 account. Remember, a purchased Microsoft 365 subscription comes with such features as a terabyte of cloud storage on OneDrive per family member and the use of Word, Outlook, PowerPoint, OneNote, and Excel in both web and desktop form, along with all new features as Microsoft releases them.

While you certainly have the option to still just use the free version, **Copilot Pro** is available as an add-on to your existing personal or family Microsoft 365 subscription as an *additional* $20/month per user. That means that if you have a family subscription, each family member needs their own individual Copilot Pro subscription.

Copilot Pro comes with its own set of features and benefits. While the free Copilot gives only nonpeak time access to GPT-4, as a paid Copilot Pro user, you can benefit from peak time use for GPT-4 with dedicated capacity just for you.

You'll also see Copilot in the desktop versions of the Microsoft 365 apps themselves, specifically Word, Excel, PowerPoint, Outlook, and OneNote (as of this publishing, Copilot Pro does not include Teams). In future chapters, I'll be illustrating how to specifically take advantage of using Copilot in these apps. For example, in Word, Copilot can help you draft documents, summarize them, or ask questions about the content within the doc itself.

Remember those image boosts in Designer? While the free version of Copilot gives you 15 daily boosts (or tokens, remember), Copilot Pro allows you to work faster by giving you 100 daily boosts to use.

Limitations of Copilot Pro

As of this publication, Copilot Pro is currently available and supported in the following languages:

- Arabic
- Chinese Simplified
- Czech
- Danish
- Dutch

- English

- Finnish

- French

- German

- Hebrew

- Hungarian

- Italian

- Japanese

- Korean

- Norwegian

- Polish

- Portuguese

- Russian

- Spanish

- Swedish

- Thai

- Turkish

Currently, Copilot in Excel is still in preview and available in English only.

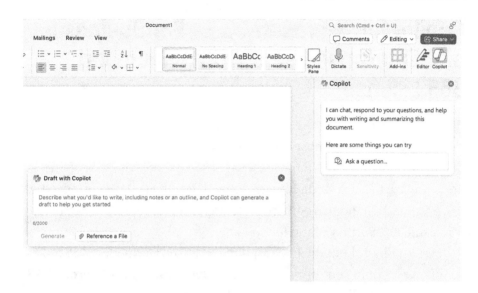

Figure 4-3. *The Copilot button on the top right will appear in the desktop versions of the apps with a paid Copilot Pro subscription for personal or family subscribers of Microsoft 365*

There are a few more limitations. From an app standpoint, Copilot Pro will currently appear in only the Windows version of **OneNote**. In all other apps, Copilot Pro will appear in both Windows *and* MacOS.

Copilot Pro does not currently support Teams.

And finally, Copilot Pro will only support certain account types in Outlook. Currently, it will support work accounts, school accounts, and Microsoft accounts using *outlook.com, hotmail.com, msn.com,* and *live.com* email addresses.

This limitation doesn't change the types of accounts you can add to Outlook. You can still use an account with IMAP or your ISP's email account or Gmail. You just won't be able to use Copilot Pro features with those accounts.

You can buy Copilot Pro at the following link or if you just prefer to see a more condensed version of the differences between the free version and Copilot Pro: `www.microsoft.com/en-us/store/b/copilotpro?rtc=1`.

Copilot for Microsoft 365 – For Business and Enterprise Users with a Microsoft 365 License

For many of you reading this book, the decision to use Copilot does not belong to you. You most likely work at a large company with an IT department that handles the who, what, when, where, and why of the apps you use to get your daily work done. In fact, you may have logged in one morning, updated your Microsoft apps, and there was Copilot for Microsoft 365. Surprise! (and lucky you!)

We've talked about the free Copilot and the home and family Copilot Pro. This remaining enterprise version is called **Copilot for Microsoft 365**.

If you're a decision maker or a smaller business wanting to take advantage of Copilot in your Microsoft tenant, here's the rundown of the current offering and requirements.

Copilot for Microsoft 365 is available as an add-on to each users' *existing* license for an *additional* $30/per user per month. While a Microsoft 365 license can be billed month to month, the licenses for Copilot for Microsoft 365 require an annual commitment and will be billed yearly.

Business customers who would like to purchase Copilot for Microsoft 365 as an add-on must be existing Microsoft 365 Business Basic, Standard, or Premium customers.

Enterprise organizations must be Microsoft 365 E3/E5/A3/A5/F1/F3 or Office 365 E1/E3/E5/A3/A5/F3 customers. There is no seat minimum *(if you heard any rumors about a 300-seat minimum to use Copilot in your organization, you are not wrong; this limitation was removed in January 2024, hurrah!)*.

Like Copilot Pro, Copilot for Microsoft 365 comes with the ability to chat with Copilot in the desktop apps and on the web. You can use Copilot with Word, PowerPoint, Excel, Outlook, Teams, Loop, and more.

You'll get that enterprise-level security, privacy, and compliance I talked about in previous chapters. Copilot is web-grounded so you'll always have up-to-date information, but it's also grounded to the Microsoft Graph. Remember our discussion in Chapter 2? The Microsoft graph is your enterprise data – emails, calendar appointments, Teams chats, etc. Copilot will integrate with all of that in your tenant, and all done according to Microsoft's Responsible AI policies.

When you use Copilot with web grounding and you're signed in with your work ID, you'll also get commercial data protection, meaning your prompts and response data will never be saved.

You'll get some additional benefits as well, one being a product called Copilot Studio. It's outside the scope of this book, but Copilot Studio is a tool that customizes and tailors Copilot to integrate with other enterprise systems you use. In fact, you can create your own copilots for use in these systems. I'll briefly cover this again in the closing chapter.

Copilot for Microsoft 365 is supported in the following languages:

- Arabic

- Chinese (Simplified)

- Czech

- Danish

- Dutch

- English

- Finnish

- French

- German

- Hebrew

- Hungarian

- Italian

- Japanese

- Korean

- Norwegian

- Polish

- Portuguese

- Russian

- Spanish

- Swedish

- Thai

- Turkish

- Ukrainian

Currently, Copilot in Excel and Planner can only be used in Chinese (Simplified), English, French, German, Italian, Japanese, Portuguese (Brazil), and Spanish

Administrators can purchase Copilot as an add-on and assign the license to users by visiting the Microsoft 365 admin center at `https://admin.microsoft.com`.

After Purchasing a Copilot for Microsoft 365 or Copilot Pro License

You have just purchased a Copilot for Microsoft 365 or Copilot Pro license, great! Now what?

In the Browser

To get started right away using Copilot in the browser apps, refresh the browser window. If you still don't see Copilot, you may need to sign out, close out of the browser completely, reopen the browser, and sign back in again.

In the Desktop Apps

Once you or your organization has successfully purchased Copilot and assigned a license to your account, you should immediately see the Copilot icon on the top right-hand side in the desktop or web versions of Excel, PowerPoint, Outlook, OneNote, and Word.

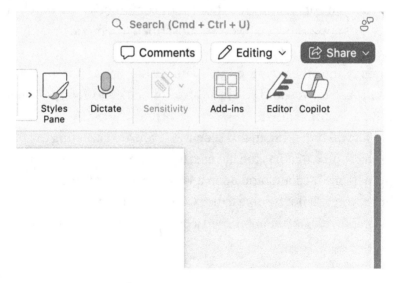

Figure 4-4. *Close-up of the Copilot icon on the top right-hand side of the desktop apps*

Sign into the Apps with the Correct Account

If you don't see the Copilot logo on the top right-hand side of your desktop apps, double-check and make sure you are signed into the apps with the same account that specifically has the license for Copilot *(remember, each family member needs their own license to use Copilot Pro)*.

Here's an important potential gotcha: If you use both a business and a personal OneDrive account on a desktop computer, Copilot will only be available to you in the app if the file you're using is stored on the account that has the license to use Copilot.

It's wonderful that you can easily switch back and forth between personal and work files on the same computer, but I did want to mention this as it could be a huge source of frustration. This scenario doesn't matter if you're opening or creating files from your computer's local hard drive.

This *only* applies to you if you've subscribed to a home or family Copilot Pro license *and* you also have your work OneDrive on the same computer, or the other way around – your employer has purchased a Copilot license for you and you have also connected to your personal OneDrive account.

Copilot will *only* work in this scenario if you are accessing the file from the correct source that has the license. If you subscribe to Copilot Pro on your personal account and open a Word document from your work OneDrive, you will not be able to use Copilot's features in that document as your employer has not purchased a license in that account and vice versa.

Update Your License in the Apps

If you're still not seeing the Copilot icon in the apps and you've verified you've logged into the right account, you also *may* need to update your license, which is just a fancy way of saying you need to force the apps to recognize the new subscription.

Mac

On a Mac, from any of the apps, click the app name to the left of the File menu and choose **Update License**.

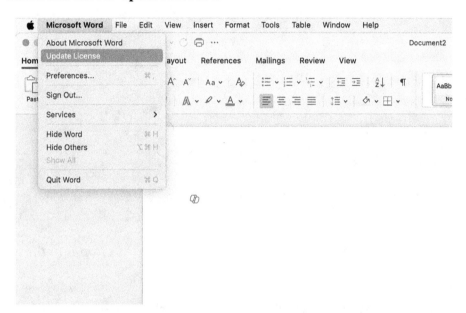

Figure 4-5. *On a Mac, update your license sign-in again if you don't see Copilot*

Windows

On a Windows computer, click **File ➤ Account**, and from there, click **Update License**.

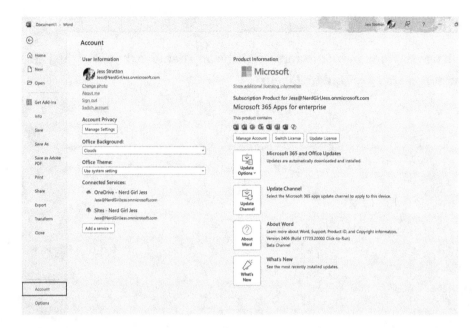

Figure 4-6. On a Windows PC, the Update License option is in the Account area

After doing this, you should also completely close out of any open Microsoft 365 apps and restart them to complete the refresh.

Curious if Your Business or Enterprise Account Is Licensed for Copilot?

If you're a business or enterprise user who does not make the decisions but are curious if you are licensed to be able to use Copilot, you can absolutely check and see for yourself what you're licensed for and entitled to use. Who knows, there may be some other apps you didn't know you could use also!

1. Log into your account on the web by visiting `www.microsoft365.com`.

2. Sign in, and then click **Home** on the left navigation bar.

3. Click **Install and more** on the right and select **Install Microsoft 365 apps** (don't worry, you're just looking; you aren't going to install anything!).

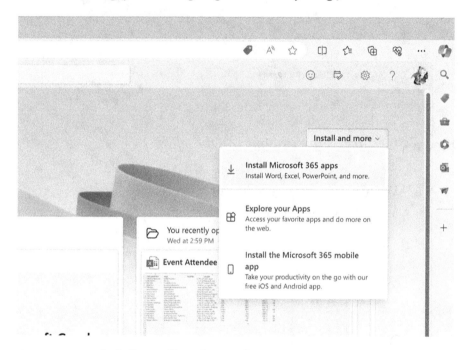

Figure 4-7. *Click "Install and more" and choose to install the apps, even though you aren't planning on installing anything*

4.   On the left, click **Subscriptions**.

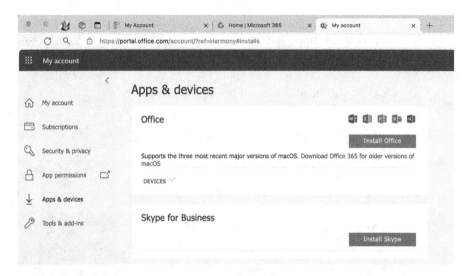

Figure 4-8. *Click "Subscriptions," on the left*

5.   Verify if you can see Copilot for Microsoft 365 listed among your subscriptions on the right.

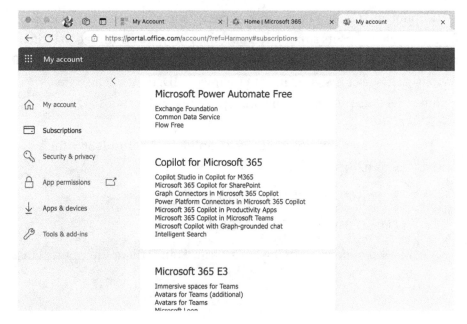

Figure 4-9. *If you see an entry for Copilot for Microsoft 365, you are a licensed user*

Up next, the fun begins. Let's dive right into using Copilot in the apps.

Summary

There are three main products and target audiences for Copilot. **Copilot** is the name given to the free web version anyone with a Microsoft account can use. **Copilot Pro** is for home and family subscribers and is an additional $20 per month per family member along with their regular Microsoft 365 subscription price. **Copilot for Microsoft 365** is for business and enterprise users and is an additional $30 per month (billed annually) per user along with the regular subscription price.

Copilot and Copilot Pro users can create and analyze images. Copilot for Microsoft 365 users *cannot* do this unless they are permitted to switch to the web-grounded tab on a browser, which I will illustrate in Chapter 10. As long as the user is signed in with their work ID, they will also get commercial data protection, meaning prompts and responses are not saved.

The following plans are eligible for Copilot for Microsoft 365, the primary focus of this book:

Microsoft 365: E3/E5/A3/A5/F1/F3

Office 365: E1/E3/E5/A3/A5/F3

Business customers with Business Basic, Standard, or Premium plans.

CHAPTER 5

Copilot in Word

You're all subscribed, you're signed in properly, and you've verified that the Copilot logo is where it's supposed to be. All signs point to go; we're ready to dive into some practical examples, ideas, and how-to's of how to use Copilot in the desktop apps! Let's start with Copilot in Word. The best part? It doesn't matter if you're using Windows or Mac; the experience is going to be the same for you.

Copilot in Word can do **four** major things:

1. It can generate content.

2. It can transform existing content by rewriting it or converting it to a table.

3. It can summarize and answer questions about existing content.

4. It can be a research tool and answer questions about existing content, something completely different, or even how to accomplish a task in Word.

Let's go over each of these tasks, and the different ways you can access Copilot in Word to accomplish them.

© Jess Stratton 2024
J. Stratton, *Copilot for Microsoft 365*, Inside Copilot,
https://doi.org/10.1007/979-8-8688-0447-2_5

Generate Content in a New, Blank Document

When you first open a new, blank document, you'll see the **Draft with Copilot** dialog box in the center of the Word document.

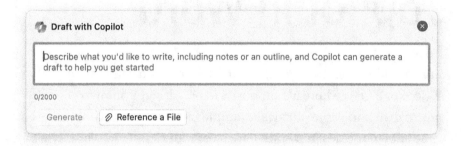

Figure 5-1. The Draft with Copilot dialog box appears in a new, blank document

This dialog box is a super fun, fast way to create content because it specifically inserts the content on the line where the cursor is. If you close out of the dialog box by accident, place the cursor on a new line and click the icon in the left margin to get it back.

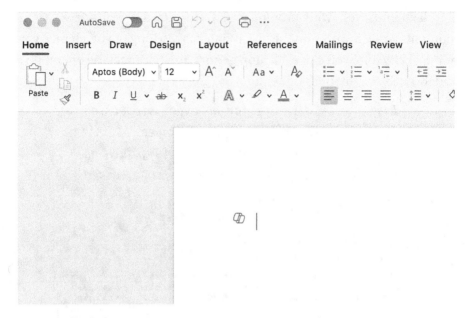

Figure 5-2. *The Copilot icon as it appears on the left margin*

Note that if you click the icon on any line that already has *existing* text, you'll get a different menu (which I'll be covering later in this chapter).

Let's start generating! For this example, I would like to create an employee handbook. We talked earlier about prompt examples; it's time to illustrate those in real-world use cases. In this specific case, I know I need to create an employee handbook, but don't really know where to start. I'm sure it needs things like vacation policies, sick leave, dress codes, and possibly a company mission (that we don't have yet).

It sounds like it's going to be a big document. That's a lot of typing and formatting. And perhaps writing such an important piece of information is out of my comfort level. That's OK. A large, blank screen can be really overwhelming. Copilot in Word can help by giving us a place to start. Let's see what it can come up with!

I'll enter the following prompt, click **Generate**, and wait a few moments while it works on the task (if it takes too long or you change your mind, at any time you can click **Stop generating** to cancel the operation, and this goes for anytime you enter a prompt).

> *I am the HR director for an event production agency. I need to create an Employee Handbook that covers important items such as vacation time, sick leave, dress code, and a work from home policy.*

Figure 5-3. *A prompt to get started creating a company handbook*

Once it's finished, the document is created, the entire chunk of generated text will be highlighted, and I'll be shown a new dialog box with some follow-up actions.

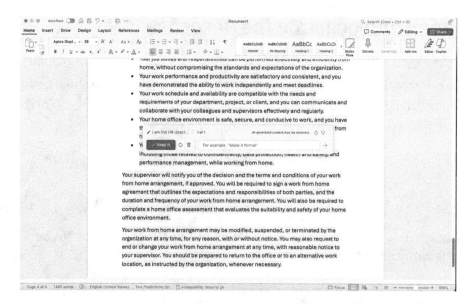

Figure 5-4. *The document is now populated, and the dialog box has changed*

Rate the Response

Right away, I want to point out the top right-hand side of the new dialog box, specifically the text that says **AI-generated content may be incorrect**, followed by a thumbs-up and thumbs-down icon. Those icons are for you to report back to Microsoft how Copilot did at responding to your prompt. It's always optional, but those icons will be there after every prompt if you'd like to report a job well done or false, misleading, offensive, or dangerous information.

Keep the Response As Is

Below that is a big blue button labeled **Keep It**, which you can click if you're happy with the results. The dialog box will go away, and the content is yours to edit and make your own.

Refresh/Regenerate the Response

To the right of that is the refresh/regenerate icon, which will completely redo the entire response, leaving the first draft available again should you choose that one instead. You can scroll through each draft at the top of the dialog box and choose to keep which one you prefer.

Figure 5-5. *Click the back arrow next to "2 of 2" to get back to the originally generated content draft*

Delete or Refine the Response

You can click the trash can icon to delete the draft entirely and start over from scratch, or you can further refine the response by including any changes you wish or additional context in the text box. Copilot already gives you an example by including the text **For example, "Make it professional".** Perhaps you want the document shorter? Longer? More precise? Less formal? Only you and your company culture can answer that one.

For now, I'm going to choose **Keep It**, and we'll add more to the document as we go through the examples and navigation.

We're left with a fully functional four-page document that Copilot completely generated for us, containing all the elements I asked for. Now I can go through and edit the document and change the specific policies to those of our fictitious event planning company.

Generate Content in an Existing Document

The **Draft with Copilot** dialog box I showed you in a new, blank document can also be used in a document with *existing* content on it by putting the insertion point on a new line. It can be anywhere in the document, as long as it's on a blank line.

I want to insert a paragraph in the *Vacation Time* section of the document, so I'll put the cursor on a new line in between the end of the section but just before the next section starts and click the Copilot icon in the left margin.

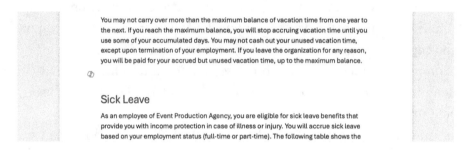

Figure 5-6. *The Copilot icon appears in the margin on any new line*

Figure 5-7. *When there's already content on the document, you'll see the addition of the Inspire Me button*

Use the Inspire Me Button

Note that there's one new button here that wasn't in the original **Draft with Copilot** dialog box, and that's the **Inspire Me** button. This button will create an additional paragraph of text related to your document to get your creative juices going!

Reference an Existing File

I'd like to include our holidays that we give our employees in this section, and I currently do have a holiday list document already saved on my OneDrive. Gone are the days of hunting down data from a long document and copying and pasting – instead, we can let Copilot find it. I'm going to prompt Copilot to insert our holidays, and this time, I'll click the **Reference a file** button (only available to Copilot for Microsoft 365 users, not Copilot Pro).

You can include up to 3 Word or PowerPoint files that Copilot can use as reference when creating content in a document. Those files can be in either your organization's SharePoint or OneDrive; however, you specifically must be able to have access to them.

A list of recently accessed files from OneDrive appears in the dropdown list; you can either choose from that or use the "/" followed by the name of the file.

My prompt now says the following:

```
Create a section titled "EMEA Holidays" and
include the EMEA table in Holidays.docx
```

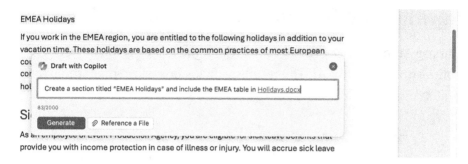

EMEA Holidays

If you work in the EMEA region, you are entitled to the following holidays in addition to your vacation time. These holidays are based on the common practices of most European

Draft with Copilot	
Create a section titled "EMEA Holidays" and include the EMEA table in Holidays.docx	

83/2000

Generate   🖉 Reference a File

As an employee of Event Production Agency, you are eligible for sick leave benefits that provide you with income protection in case of illness or injury. You will accrue sick leave

Figure 5-8. *Copilot can add content based on a referenced file from OneDrive or SharePoint*

Referencing a file using Copilot isn't just for inserting content, it's also made for matching tone and writing style. I encourage you to play around with this feature; it may end up being one of your favorites!

Transforming Existing Content

When you highlight existing text and click the Copilot icon in the left margin, you'll get some different options.

Work from Home Policy

As an employee of Event Production Agency, you may have the option to work from home, either on a regular or occasional basis, depending on your job duties, performance, and availability. Working from home is a flexible work arrangement that allows you to perform your work remotely, using technology and communication tools, while maintaining the quality and quantity of your output. Working from home is not a right or a benefit, but a privilege that may be granted or revoked by the organization at any time, for any reason.

Write a Prompt...

Auto Rewrite

Visualize as a Table

Services   >

...ork from home, you must submit a written request to your supervisor, ...ons, the frequency, and the duration of your desired work from home ...our supervisor will review your request and evaluate your eligibility based on ...iteria:

- Your job duties and responsibilities can be performed effectively and efficiently from home, without compromising the standards and expectations of the organization.

Figure 5-9. *Selecting text and clicking the Copilot icon in the margin will give you different options*

Rewrite with Copilot

Choose **Auto Rewrite** to have your highlighted text be given new rewrites courtesy of generative AI. The resulting dialog box will contain three new drafts you can scroll through by clicking the arrows at the top.

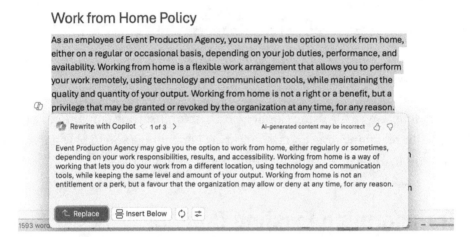

Figure 5-10. *Rewriting existing content with Copilot will let you choose from three new generated drafts and replace it outright or insert it below the original text*

The bottom menu contains your actions.

Replace or Insert As Additional Text

You can use the blue **Replace** button to replace the existing text with any of the three drafts you choose.

If you'd rather not lose the existing text but decide later which draft you want, you can instead choose **Insert Below** to drop the draft below the existing highlighted text.

Regenerate or Change the Tone of the Response

You can click the refresh/regenerate icon to get three entirely new drafts to choose from.

Finally, you can click the icon with the two lines to change the overall tone of the rewrite. Once you select a desired tone (the default is neutral, but you can choose professional, casual, imaginative, or concise), click **Regenerate** to get three new drafts, and you can replace the text with your choice or begin the process all over again.

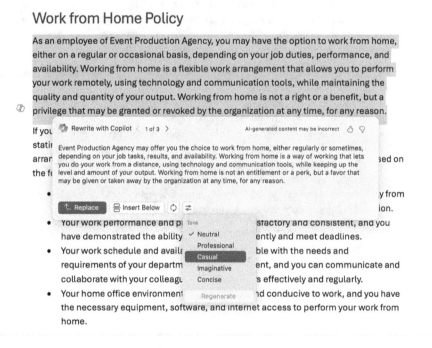

Figure 5-11. *You can change the tone of the rewrite by choosing from the menu*

Transform Text into a Table

There's one more task you can accomplish with the Copilot icon in the margin, and that's transforming selected text into a table.

Highlight your text, click the Copilot icon in the left margin, and choose **Visualize as a Table**. The resulting dialog box should be familiar to you now. You can keep it, regenerate it for new options, trash it, or refine it.

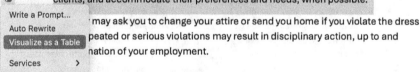

Dress Code

As an employee of Event Production Agency, you are expected to dress in a professional and appropriate manner that reflects the image and reputation of the organization. You should also consider the nature of your work, the safety of yourself and others, and the expectations of your clients and partners. The following guidelines apply to all employees, regardless of their employment status or position:

- You should wear clean, neat, and well-fitting clothing that is suitable for your work environment and activities.
- You should avoid wearing clothing that is excessively casual, revealing, provocative, offensive, or inappropriate for the workplace.
- You should follow the specific dress code requirements of your department, project, or client, if any.
- You should wear protective clothing and equipment, such as gloves, helmets, or masks, when required by your job or by law.
- You should respect the cultural and religious diversity of your colleagues and clients, and accommodate their preferences and needs, when possible.

Write a Prompt...
Auto Rewrite
Visualize as a Table
Services   >

may ask you to change your attire or send you home if you violate the dress peated or serious violations may result in disciplinary action, up to and nation of your employment.

Figure 5-12. Copilot can convert text to a table for you

In this example, I've decided a table will break up the text and make a longer document easier on the eyes to read. The workplace attire guidelines have been successfully converted into a table format; however, I think it can still look better and be easier to read. I'll refine the results by telling Copilot to remove the words "you should" from the table.

Workplace Attire Guidelines

You should wear clean, neat, and well-fitting clothing that is suitable for your work environment and activities.

You should avoid wearing clothing that is excessively casual, revealing, provocative, offensive, or inappropriate for the workplace.

You sho ... , or client, i

You sho ... sks, when re

You should respect the cultural and religious diversity of your colleagues and clients, and accommodate their preferences and needs, when possible.

> ‹ To fine tune the draft, add some detail and regenerate
>
> Remove the words "you should" →
>
> Generate

Figure 5-13. *You can refine the table, for example, by changing words or adding columns*

Tables are a wonderful way to visualize data, and Copilot does a great job of breaking that data into columns and rows. Here's one more example where Copilot converted text into a table. I could refine this by telling it to make a certain column wider or shorter or add a blank column.

Full time employees have an accrual rate of 12 days per year, with 24 days as a maximum balance. Part time employees have an accrual rate of 6 days per year with a maximum balance of 12 days.

Write a Prompt...

Auto Rewrite

Visualize as a Table

Services   ›

Figure 5-14. *This data could be more easily digested if it was in table format*

Employee Type	Accrual Rate (Days/Year)	Maximum Balance (Days)
Full Time	12	24
Part Time	6	12

Figure 5-15. *The resulting table is much easier to read*

Summarize and Get Questions Answered About Existing Content

We're all done talking about the Copilot icon in the left margin and ready to start tackling the big Copilot icon on the top right-hand side of the Home ribbon!

Figure 5-16. *Clicking the Copilot icon on the top right-hand side of the document will open a sidebar pane*

Clicking the icon brings up a pane on the right-hand side of the document. If you open it by accident or wish to close it, click the **X** in the top right-hand side of the pane. Click the Copilot icon at any time to reopen it.

This area of Copilot is much more powerful and flexible than using Copilot in the margin. You can summarize the document, get questions answered about its contents, or generate text. The first time you open the pane, you'll notice that it's divided into two distinct sections:

1. The top section contains some ideas in the form of action buttons that Copilot has given you to get started.

2. The bottom section contains a prompt window with some additional icons.

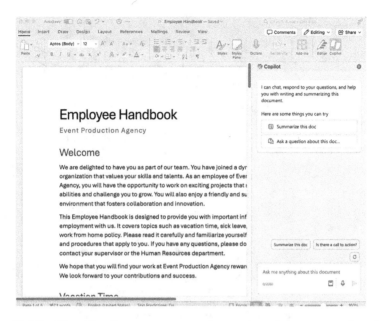

Figure 5-17. *The Copilot pane contains action buttons and a chat area at the bottom*

Summarize the Document

If you open a new, blank document, the button at the top will most likely say "Ask a question." However, since we already have content on the document, I get some more options. If I choose the **Summarize this document** action button, I'll get a bulleted list of main ideas with citations within the document. I can click the numbered citations underneath each point to see where Copilot has gathered the information from.

Revise the Summary

And, like all responses, I am once again given the option to revise. I can see three more options in the form of buttons – **Expand on the main point in the summary**, **Make the summary more casual**, and of course the refresh icon which will completely regenerate the response. These options will change depending on what you're asking Copilot to do for you.

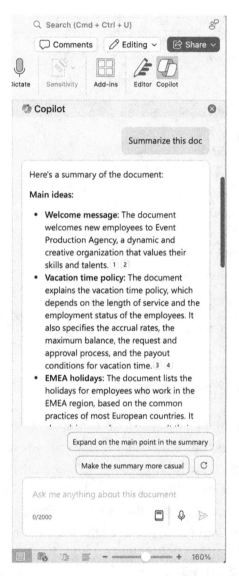

Figure 5-18. *Copilot has summarized a long document for me directly in the pane*

I do want to back up a bit – there are some more options that are easy to miss, especially when the response is long enough to make you scroll through the pane. I'm going to scroll all the way to the end of the summary response.

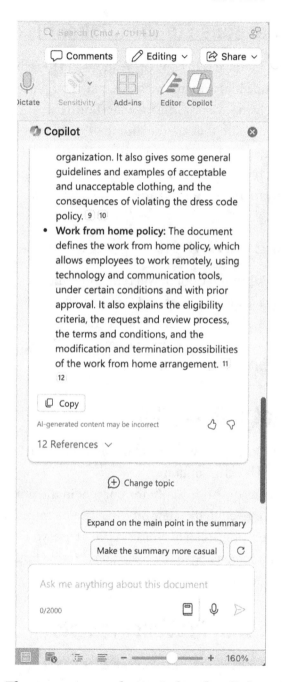

Figure 5-19. *The response can be copied to the clipboard; you can view the citations or change the topic to start a new chat*

Copy the Response to the Clipboard

The first choice you have is to copy the response to the clipboard – perhaps you want to include it in a Teams message, email, or paste it into a new document entirely to save on OneDrive for future use.

Directly underneath that are the thumbs-up/thumbs-down review buttons, and underneath that is an expandable list of all the references Copilot used to create the summary. You can click on each link which will take you directly to the referenced area in the document.

Change to a New Topic

Chatting in Word through Copilot will remember the context of your chats, so you can keep asking questions and Copilot will answer in context with what you were previously chatting about. However, should you want to start fresh with a new conversation, you can click **Change topic**, right underneath the previous responses to start over.

Start a Chat with Copilot

Let's talk about the prompt window at the bottom of the Copilot pane. This is how you can chat with Copilot.

You can ask any question about the content in the prompt window, and if you want or need to dictate, you can click the microphone icon to speak your prompt instead of typing. As you type, you'll notice a character count increasing in the dialog box. You're limited to a 2,000-character prompt.

Get Started with Prebuilt Prompts

Should you need a starting point, you can click on the **View Prompts** icon to open a catalog of prompt foundations you can get started with.

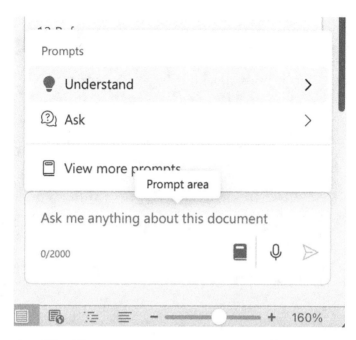

Figure 5-20. *The View Prompts menu option will get you started with sample prompts and can take you to Copilot Lab, a Microsoft web page to view more tips and tricks*

View Starter Prompts to Understand Your Document or Ask Questions About the Content

The **Understand** and **Ask** sections will contain starting points about getting to know the existing content, and you can take the words in brackets and replace them with phrases that will be meaningful to you to gain insight about the document.

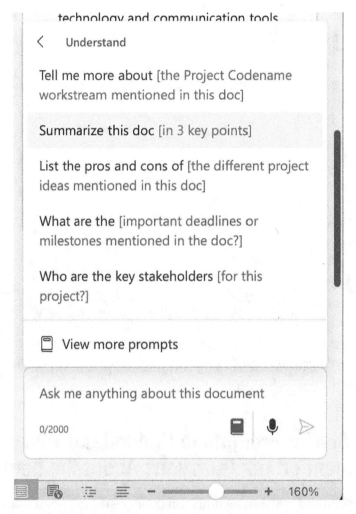

Figure 5-21. *The Understand section contains prompts in which you can replace the bracketed text with your own*

View More Prompts Online at Copilot Lab

Clicking **View more prompts** will open a new window containing even more prompts you can try. It's called Copilot Lab, and you can click **See all prompts in Copilot Lab** at the bottom of the screen to open a Microsoft website containing tips, tricks, and more prompts you can try to help get your work done faster.

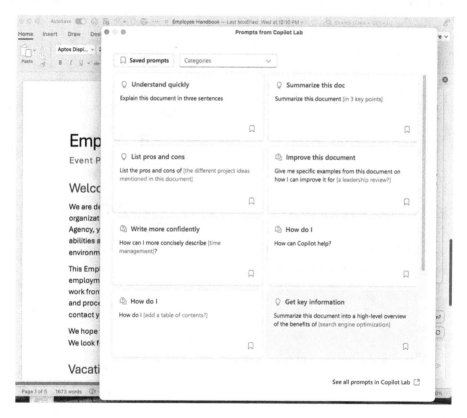

Figure 5-22. *Copilot Lab is chock-full of sample prompts to help you get the most out of your document*

87

Research and Get Questions Answered While You're Using Word

You can ask anything about the document, but also so much more. I can ask research questions about the topic I'm writing on, or anything. In this case, while I'm scrolling through the document and reading about the employee holiday schedule, I may wonder to myself what the history of Boxing Day is. I have but to ask.

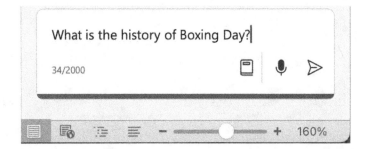

Figure 5-23. *I can do research directly by chatting with Copilot*

Note that Copilot reminds me that the response isn't based on any content in the document itself.

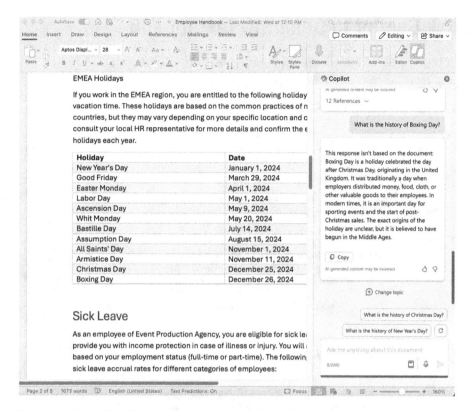

Figure 5-24. *Copilot reminds me that its response is not based on contents in the document*

Also, note that I have the option to copy the response, should I want to paste it somewhere. This is useful for asking for stakeholder research *(what are some key benefits of working from home?)*, or for including key takeaways that I can copy and place at the end of the document *(create three summarized bullet points of the document's main topics)*. It's also useful in case I get hungry while writing the document and want to ask Copilot for a recipe for chocolate chip cookies. It could happen! Even Microsoft uses this one as an example in Copilot Lab.

Ask Copilot to Generate Text for You

Copilot in Word can also help create questions about your document. In this example, based on our handbook, I've just asked it to create a three-question multiple-choice quiz for new employees.

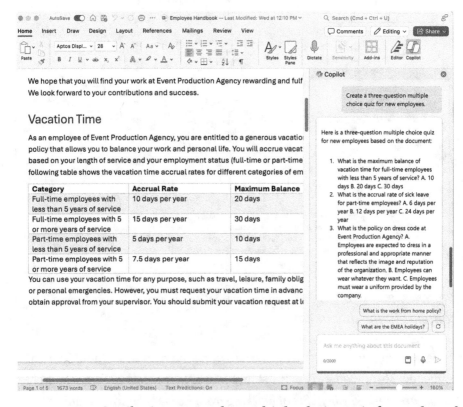

Figure 5-25. *Copilot just created a multiple-choice quiz for me based on the document*

Imagine if you had Copilot create a job description for you, complete with job title, salary range, and necessary skills. Perhaps you already had a document open that contained a new role for your organization. With that document open, you could then ask Copilot to create interview questions for you. I may be able to show you how to use Copilot, but the true value in it will be how you discover ways that it can help you in your specific line of work.

We've finally explored *just about* all the features of using Copilot in Word. To sum up, we

- Started a blank document using the **Draft with Copilot** dialog box

- Made revisions, if necessary

- Learned about the **Inspire Me** button to get additional related content added to the document

- Inserted more content by **referencing a different file** that was already on OneDrive

- Transformed existing text by highlighting it and **rewriting it with Copilot**

- Transformed existing **text into table** format

- **Summarized** the contents of the document

- Did some **research** on related topics (and not so related)

- **Created questions** based on the document using chat prompts

Get Help Using Word

There's one more thing you can use the prompt window for, and that's to ask Copilot how to use Word! You could ask Copilot how to create columns in the document, how to do a mail merge, how to create a table of contents, and more. Forget sifting through the help files, next time you need to accomplish a task, just ask Copilot in Word.

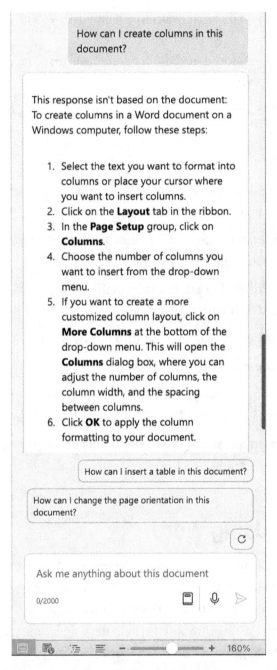

Figure 5-26. *You can easily ask Copilot how to accomplish a task in Word itself*

Up next, let's dive into using Copilot in Excel.

Summary

Copilot in Word can generate content for you based on a prompt. You can then revise or regenerate content and choose which draft you'd prefer to start working with. You can also transform existing content by rewriting it or converting it into a table.

You can use the Copilot icon on the toolbar to open a sidebar pane to use more features of Copilot. From this pane, you can summarize a long document or get questions answered about existing content, complete with citations within the Word document itself.

Finally, Copilot in Word can be used as a research tool to answer general questions, compose questions and answers, or even to accomplish a task in Word.

CHAPTER 6

Copilot in Excel

As we progress through the chapters now that we're finally *using* Copilot hands-on, you'll begin to notice that it works the same way in certain apps and a bit different in other apps. When it's the same, the familiarity will help you learn and use Copilot more effectively. For example, you'll begin to look for the action buttons at the top of the Copilot pane that opens on the right-hand side of the apps, and you'll also know that the prompt window to start a chat is on the bottom of the pane.

Copilot in Excel works much the same way as it did in Word, so I'll also start in much the same way and tell you the four major things that Copilot can do with your Excel data:

1. It can identify data insights for you in the form of charts, PivotTables, summaries, trends, and outliers.

2. It can transform data by highlighting, sorting, filtering, and formatting it.

3. It can create column formulas for you and explain how they work.

4. It can be a research tool and answer questions about your data, something completely different, or even how to accomplish a task in Excel.

However, unlike with Word, opening a new Excel workbook does *not* open a Copilot dialog box in the center of the screen. To use Copilot in Excel, you must click the **Copilot** button on the Home ribbon tab.

© Jess Stratton 2024
J. Stratton, *Copilot for Microsoft 365*, Inside Copilot,
https://doi.org/10.1007/979-8-8688-0447-2_6

As of this publishing, Copilot in Excel is still in preview, so you'll see "(Preview)" after the Copilot header. That's perfectly normal and you aren't doing anything wrong or missing any features. The Copilot team is working hard to add new features and release Copilot for Excel in more languages.

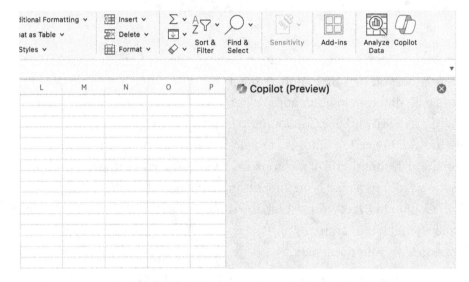

Figure 6-1. *Copilot for Excel is still in preview mode, so seeing (Preview) is perfectly normal*

Download the Sample File Used in This Chapter

I have created an Excel file using data to explore Copilot's capabilities that I'll be using for the examples in this chapter. While absolutely not required, if you'd like to follow along with the same prompts while you read, I have made the file available to you as a download from my website at www.nerdgirljess.com/downloads.

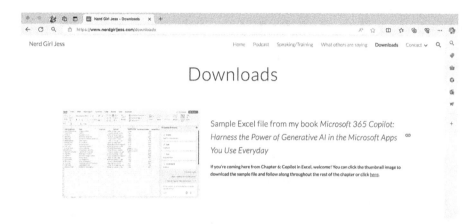

Figure 6-2. *Click the image to download the sample file used in this chapter if you'd like to follow along*

Unlike the other apps, Copilot in Excel has some prerequisites, so if you're struggling to make it work, make sure to revisit this checklist and make sure your workbook meets the following requirements:

Turn On AutoSave

Your file **must** be stored on OneDrive, SharePoint, or local machines with OneDrive Sync and AutoSave turned on. In fact, if you open a new, blank workbook and click the **Copilot** button, you'll see that it's even offering to do it for you right in the pane.

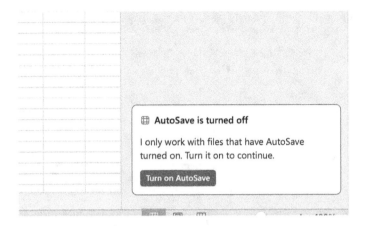

Figure 6-3. *AutoSave must be turned on before you can use Copilot in Excel*

To use AutoSave, your file *must* be stored on OneDrive or SharePoint, so you'll be prompted to save it to a folder on your Microsoft 365's OneDrive account.

If your file is already on OneDrive, it's possible that AutoSave still might be turned off for that particular file, so you can toggle it back on at the very top of the ribbon.

If you've downloaded the sample file, remember that you'll need to upload it to OneDrive or SharePoint and make sure AutoSave is on before continuing.

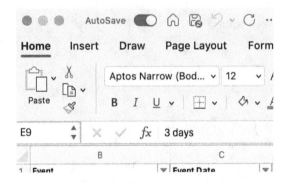

Figure 6-4. *Even if your file is already saved on OneDrive, AutoSave might still be turned off. Make sure the toggle button is green*

Select Any Cell That Contains Data from an Excel Table or Data Range

Once your Excel workbook is stored on OneDrive or SharePoint and AutoSave is turned on, you're *almost* ready to use Copilot in Excel, but there's one more gotcha that's easy to miss.

A cell containing data **must** be selected. That data can be in an Excel table, or from a data range. You don't have to specifically do anything to create that range, as long as your data meets the following specifications:

- It contains a header row with different column names.

- There are no empty rows or columns (I like to click inside my dataset and type **CTRL + .** repeatedly to navigate through the four corners of the range to make sure there are no gaps).

- It has consistent data formatting per column.

- There are no subtotals in the range.

(Optionally) Format your data as an Excel table.

If you'd like to format your data as a table, you can absolutely do that. If you've never used an Excel table before, it's a great way to manage large amounts of data cohesively and easily. Formatting your data as an Excel table doesn't change or rearrange your data; instead, it adds tools such as filters and total rows. It visually bands the data making it easier to read, and when you add or remove data to the table, it will automatically increase or decrease the range and update any PivotTables or totals with the new values.

To create a table, you need to make sure you have no empty rows, which is already a requirement to use Copilot in Excel. Again, I like to click inside the data and type **CTRL + .** repeatedly to navigate through the four corners of the range to make sure there are no gaps and all the data I want is contained.

Make sure there is a header row, and then click any cell inside the range. From the Home ribbon tab, click **Format as table**, and then choose a table style. Instantly you'll see the rows banded with the color you chose, and filter buttons will appear at the right edge of each header column.

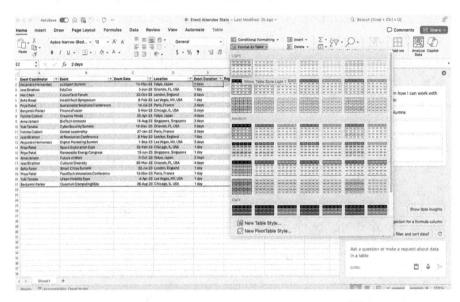

Figure 6-5. *I have created an Excel table for my fictional company to analyze with Copilot for Excel. You can download this at* `www.nerdgirljess.com/downloads`

Once your file meets all the criteria or you've formatted your data as an Excel table, you need to make sure you've selected a cell (any cell) in the table or range before clicking the **Copilot** icon.

Why is this so easy to miss? Because while Copilot was incredibly helpful in reminding me that I needed to turn AutoSave on, it **won't** tell me that it needs to select a cell first. In Figure 6-6, notice that the highlighted cell is *outside* the table or range.

2 days	5642	5642	$	1,500
2 days	376	376	$	3,700
1 day	9658	9000	$	50
2 days	3174	2300	$	200
1 day	6945	6400	$	50
1 day	1826	1524	$	-
2 days	5023	5023	$	890
4 days	831	800	$	20
1 day	4259	3500	$	-
1 day	7602	7540	$	500
1 day	548	547	$	800
1 day	9251	7032	$	200

No data selected from an Excel table or data range

I only work with data in Excel tables or data ranges with the following criteria:

- a single header row with different column names
- no empty rows or columns
- consistent data formatting per column
- no subtotals

Try selecting data that meets the criteria or is formatted as a table (**Insert > Table**).

Ask a question or make a request about data in a table

Figure 6-6. *Gotcha warning! Copilot tells me that my data needs to be in an Excel table, but all I need to do is make sure I have selected a cell inside the existing table*

Once I click any cell *inside* the table or range, the Copilot pane finally behaves as expected and I can see some action buttons at the top to get me started and the prompt window at the bottom.

Figure 6-7. *When AutoSave is turned on and the active cursor is in a cell containing data, the Copilot pane shows action buttons and the prompt window*

101

Just to reiterate one more time, before you can use Copilot, these three prerequisites must be met:

- Your Excel workbook is stored on OneDrive or SharePoint and AutoSave is turned on.

- Your data has been formatted as an Excel table or has no empty rows or columns in the range.

- A cell, any cell, has been selected inside the table.

Let's go play with Copilot in Excel!

Identify Insights
Summaries, Trends, and Outliers

Copilot in Excel can not only identify a particular insight you're looking for, but it can also come up with some of its own and give you some insights you may not have realized were right there in the data waiting to be discovered.

The four action buttons at the top are consistent in Excel regardless of what workbook you have open and what type of data is in your table.

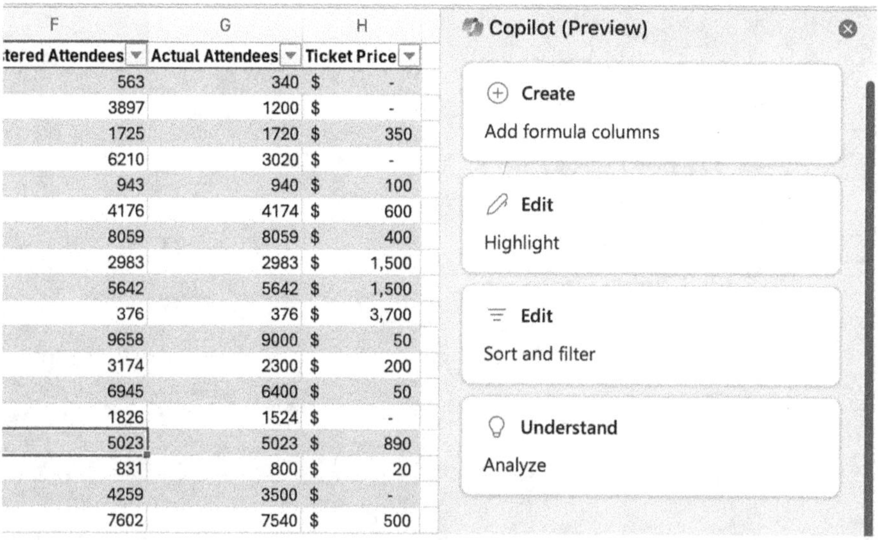

F	G	H
tered Attendees ▼	Actual Attendees ▼	Ticket Price ▼
563	340	$ -
3897	1200	$ -
1725	1720	$ 350
6210	3020	$ -
943	940	$ 100
4176	4174	$ 600
8059	8059	$ 400
2983	2983	$ 1,500
5642	5642	$ 1,500
376	376	$ 3,700
9658	9000	$ 50
3174	2300	$ 200
6945	6400	$ 50
1826	1524	$ -
5023	5023	$ 890
831	800	$ 20
4259	3500	$ -
7602	7540	$ 500

Copilot (Preview)   ⊗

⊕ **Create**

Add formula columns

✎ **Edit**

Highlight

≡ **Edit**

Sort and filter

♡ **Understand**

Analyze

Figure 6-8. *The four action buttons will always be there to get you started in Excel*

As you can see in Figure 6-8, you can **add formula columns**, **highlight**, **sort and filter**, and **analyze** your data. Clicking the **Understand/Analyze** button will create some basic prompts I can choose.

This workbook contains events that my fictional event production agency has put on recently. It contains data such as the event date, duration, location, how many registered attendees we had, and how many total people attended the event.

The **Understand/Analyze** button suggests some prompts to get me started, and I can click the refresh/regenerate icon to get some more ideas of ways to analyze my data. If you're following along, it's important to note that Copilot may give you different suggested prompts than what you see in the figures.

Figure 6-9. *Clicking Analyze will give me some prompt samples I can start with to give me insight into my data*

Just like Word, Copilot in Excel has a button to view prompts you can click to view some inspiration prompts and add in your own column header values.

Figure 6-10. *Viewing prompts can teach you things you can ask Copilot for Excel as well as get you started with some ideas*

For example, if I click inside **Understand**, I can click on "**How many different [teams are represented in this table]**". The prompt gets populated with everything before the brackets, and I can replace those with column header data that will be meaningful to my own analysis.

Figure 6-11. *You can read the text in brackets and type in your own data's unique column headers*

I have a column for the names of the event coordinators, so if I ask Copilot how many different event coordinators are represented in this table, I can see that it returns a calculated value that I could choose to add to a new sheet (it's actually a PivotTable, but we'll talk about that in a moment). As always, I have the warning about AI-generated content followed by the thumbs-up/thumbs-down rating system, and it's also given me a response in plain text that I can copy to the clipboard.

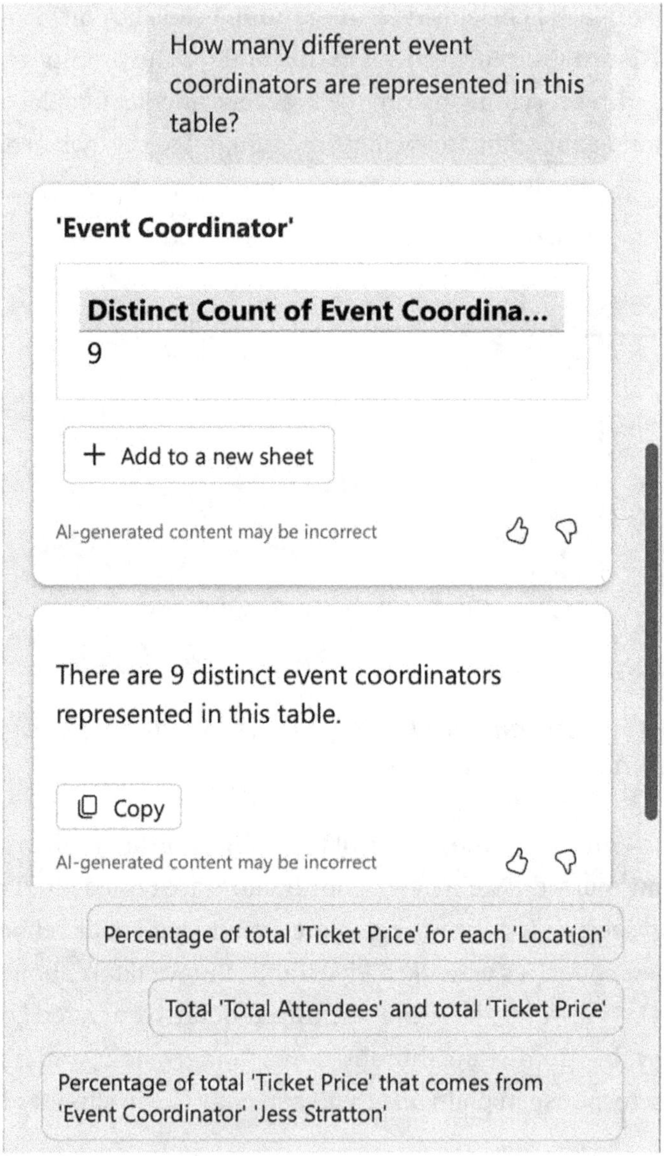

How many different event coordinators are represented in this table?

'Event Coordinator'

Distinct Count of Event Coordina...
9

+ Add to a new sheet

AI-generated content may be incorrect

There are 9 distinct event coordinators represented in this table.

Copy

AI-generated content may be incorrect

Percentage of total 'Ticket Price' for each 'Location'

Total 'Total Attendees' and total 'Ticket Price'

Percentage of total 'Ticket Price' that comes from 'Event Coordinator' 'Jess Stratton'

Figure 6-12. *I have the choice to put the response data in a new sheet or copy the response text to the clipboard*

You can always create your own prompt to ask Copilot anything about your data. If I ask Copilot **which location has the largest number of total attendees**, like the previous example, I can take the results and use them elsewhere if I so desire.

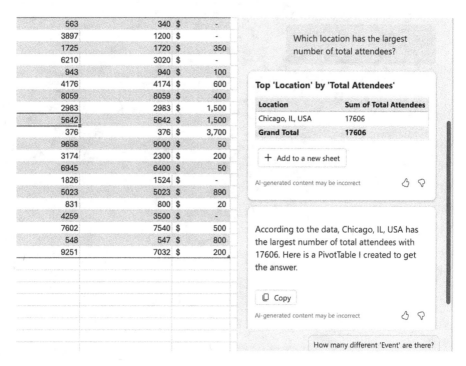

Figure 6-13. *I can always type in my own prompt in the window at any time*

Charts and PivotTables

When you ask Copilot to analyze your data, it will return its analysis in the form of PivotTables and PivotCharts. Copilot can create these charts for you based on answering questions or using action buttons, but you can also directly ask for a chart containing the data you'd like to see plotted.

In this example, I'll ask Copilot to **show me a bar chart of the top five locations based on registered attendees and include the total attendees also.**

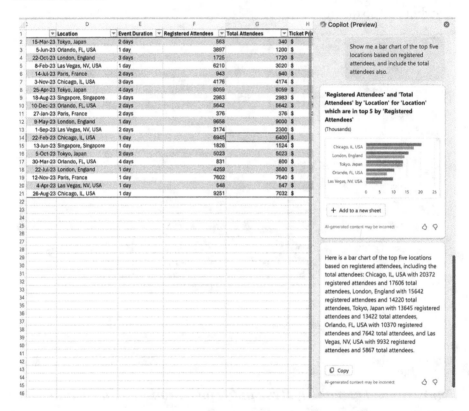

Figure 6-14. *Copilot in Excel has given me the bar chart I asked for with the option to add it to a new sheet*

Copilot gives me what I asked for, and I can click to add it to a new sheet. It's then I can see that Copilot has created a PivotChart, a chart based off data in a PivotTable that Copilot created first to fulfill my request.

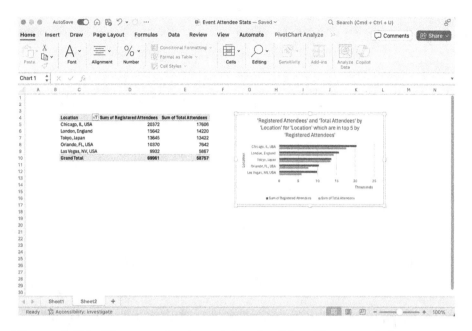

Figure 6-15. *The new sheet contains the PivotChart and the PivotTable that the chart data is based on, all created by Copilot*

PivotTables and PivotCharts are wonderful ways to analyze data, as you can play around to your heart's content without the fear of accidentally altering your original dataset, which remains safe and sound on its own worksheet. And once you have that chart, it's yours to print out or perhaps insert into a PowerPoint presentation.

You can also create a PivotTable directly, without asking for the chart beforehand. I don't even need to specify that I'm asking for a PivotTable, I can just ask to see the data I'm looking for.

`Show me the total attendees by location and event month.`

If I click to add the resulting PivotTable to a new sheet, I'll get something like this:

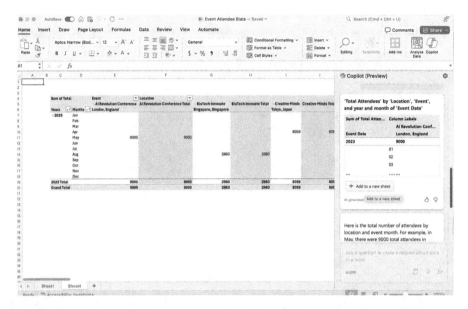

Figure 6-16. *I don't have to specifically ask for a PivotTable, but Copilot can create one anyway. After adding it to a new sheet, I can then edit it any way I choose*

There's still some work to be done on it, but you'll notice right away that Copilot has broken down the total attendees by month, just as I asked. I do have a column in my spreadsheet called **Event Date**. Copilot is smart enough to break it down into individual months without me needing to create any formulas on my part.

Transform Data

Boldface and Highlight Data

Copilot can boldface, highlight, sort, and filter your data to make it easier to read and see patterns. It can change the color of cells, or entire columns. Just as we did with our PivotTable, the easiest way is to simply ask!

Here in the following figure, I've asked Copilot to **boldface the top three events with the highest total attendees.**

:ered Attendees ▼	Total Attendees ▼	Ticket
563	340	$
3897	1200	$
1725	1720	$
6210	3020	$
943	940	$
4176	4174	$
8059	**8059**	$
2983	2983	$
5642	5642	$
376	376	$
9658	**9000**	$
3174	2300	$
6945	6400	$
1826	1524	$
5023	5023	$
831	800	$
4259	3500	$
7602	**7540**	$
5⌐⌐8	5⌐⌐7	$

Boldface the top three events with the highest total attendees.

Done! I made the following changes: I bolded and applied a black font color to the top 3 items in the column(s) 'Total Attendees'.

↺ Undo   ⎘ Copy

AI-generated content may be incorrect   👍 👎

⊕ Change topic

Show items with 'Event' of 'echXpert Summit'

Figure 6-17. Copilot in Excel can boldface values, whether they are outliers, all the same value, or any figure you need to stand out quickly

I could also have asked to **highlight** the events instead of boldface; you can see the difference it makes visually in the following figure.

Registered Attendees ▾	Total Attendees ▾	Ticket
563	340	$
3897	1200	$
1725	1720	$
6210	3020	$
943	940	$
4176	4174	$
8059	8059	$
2983	2983	$
5642	5642	$
376	376	$
9658	9000	$
3174	2300	$
6945	6400	$
1826	1524	$
5023	5023	$
831	800	$
4259	3500	$
7602	7540	$
548	547	$
9251	7032	$

AI-generated content may be incorrect

Highlight the top three events with the highest total attendees.

Done! I made the following changes: I applied a green fill color and a black font color to the top 3 items in the column(s) 'Total Attendees'.

Undo   Copy

AI-generated content may be incorrect

(+) Change topic

Show items with 'Event Duration' of '2 days'

Bold the first column

Figure 6-18. *The same prompt, except this time the cells are highlighted in addition to the boldface*

It's important to note that Copilot uses conditional formatting to perform these tasks, which means that adding additional rows at any time could make these highlighted or boldfaced values change dynamically as the data changes.

Sort and Filter Data

When you type your prompt to Copilot for sorting and filtering, you absolutely can and should use the identical text that's in your header column, but you can also experiment with something *close* to what the exact text is.

For example, if I wanted to sort the data by event date, I might ask Copilot to **sort date by earliest to latest**. You'll notice in the results that Copilot has correctly assumed I meant the Event Date column. However, I wouldn't be able to do this, or I may get inaccurate results if I have more than one column that contains dates.

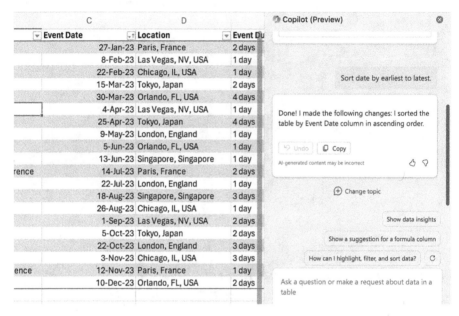

Figure 6-19. *Copilot can sort a column for you. It's best if you use the exact column name, though as you can see in this example it worked as this is the only date column*

In addition to sorting, you'll probably also spend some time filtering through your data. I mentioned earlier how a popular reason for creating an Excel table is for the automatic appearance of the filter buttons at the top of the header columns. While you absolutely can still manually create your own filters for analysis, Copilot can also filter (and unfilter) the data for you. For example, perhaps I want to see just the event data by a particular event coordinator.

113

Here, I've asked Copilot to **filter events by Jess Stratton**, and it's only showing me those events. Don't forget, you can (and should) always look in the Copilot pane to see the reasoning behind the results.

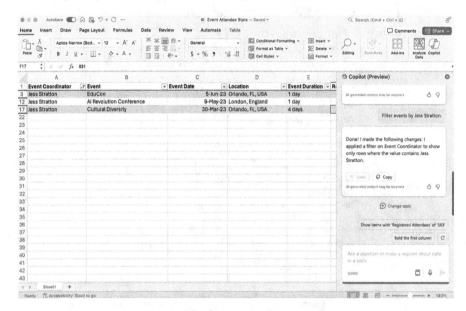

Figure 6-20. *Copilot can also filter column data*

Figure 6-21. *After the filter, you should check Copilot's logic and reasoning to make sure the filter has been applied correctly*

Create Column Formulas

In addition to answering questions about your data and highlighting outliers and requested data, Copilot in Excel really shines when it comes to adding new columns. You don't need to know how to create column formulas; you just need to know how to *ask* for them.

Let's do one more example in my event spreadsheet. I have a column containing the total number of people registered for an event and the total number of people that attended. If I wanted to find out the percentage of people that showed up, I could ask Copilot to **create a column containing the percentage of people that attended the event versus the amount that registered for it.**

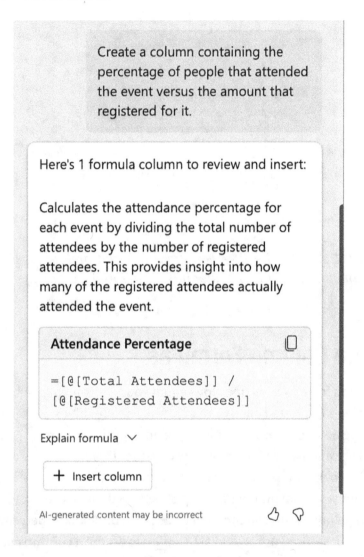

Figure 6-22. Copilot has been asked to create a column based on a formula, and it will both explain the logic and provide the text of the formula for your review

Not only will Copilot create the column formula, it will also explain how it works and display the formula itself. Not only can this help you get your work done, but it's also a fantastic learning tool. If you need more help figuring out what's going on, you can click **Explain formula** for a more thorough breakdown of what Excel has done.

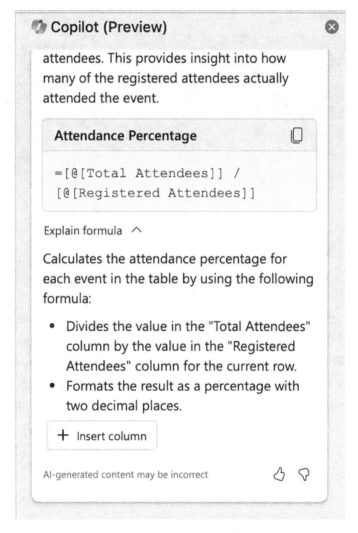

Figure 6-23. Expanding "Explain formula" will break it down into steps

You can hover your mouse over the **Insert column** button to preview the results in the worksheet itself. If the results are what you expected, click the button to add it to your sheet.

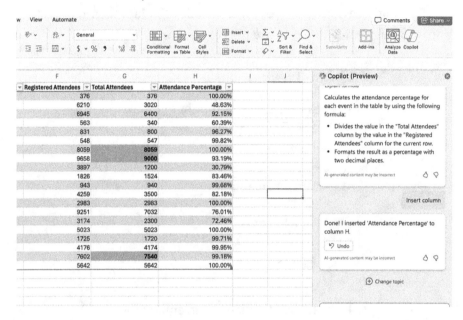

Figure 6-24. *The calculated column is added at the end of the table*

You can always format the data here as well, for instance, you may choose to remove the decimal values and round the percentage.

I'm going to move on to some new data. While I don't have a separate file for this one, it's easy enough to create on your own. It's a simple sheet with a few *first name*, *last name*, and *department* columns. I'd like to have a column with the first and last names combined to make a full name column. I'll ask Copilot to **combine the first and last names to make a full name column.**

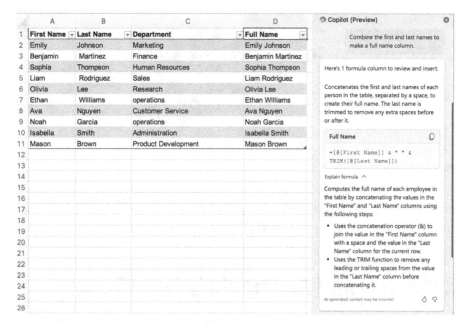

Figure 6-25. *Copilot can combine data in columns, such as the first and last name shown here*

Copilot has successfully created the formula for me, so I've inserted it into my sheet. You can see the formula along with the explanation expanded in the pane.

Let's try this one last time, except we will make it a little more complex. I need a solid list of employee names and departments that I can copy to the clipboard. I'm not able to paste in a three-column spreadsheet, however. It must be in a single column that I can copy and paste from there.

I'll type the following prompt: **Combine the first and last names to make a full name, then add a hyphen and add the department to the column.**

After previewing the data and adding it to my sheet, I'm left with the following that I can copy and paste where I need to.

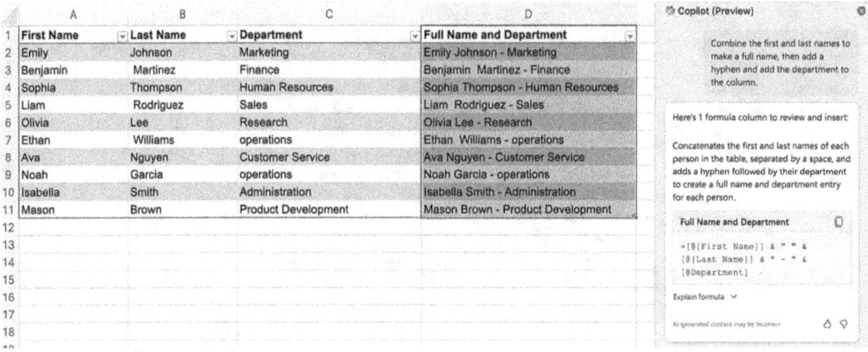

Figure 6-26. *Here is a more complex version of combining columns, complete with a hyphen as a delimiter*

Research and Accomplish Excel Tasks

We've used Copilot in Excel to analyze our data and give us insights we may not have seen before. We used it to create PivotTables and PivotCharts to visually arrange our data, highlight and boldface outliers, and sort our data. We've used it to add filters to only see what we need to be looking for at that moment, and we've added column formulas to get our work done faster.

Finally, we can use Copilot in Excel in the same way we used it in Word. We can ask random questions in the prompt box that may or may not have to do with our data, and we can ask how to accomplish a certain task in Excel.

For example, based on our last worksheet example, I might wonder what the Operations department entails. It doesn't matter that I'm in Excel – I can still ask.

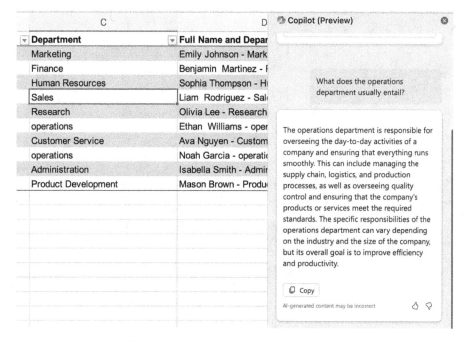

Figure 6-27. *Copilot in Excel can still answer research questions*

If I'm not sure how to perform an operation in Excel, just like we did with Word, I can ask Copilot.

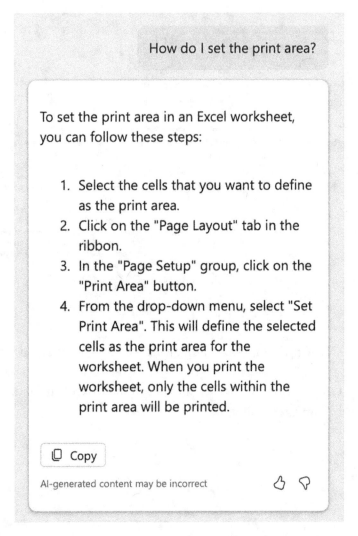

Figure 6-28. *Copilot can also answer questions about accomplishing tasks in Excel*

Up next, let's use Copilot to create presentations, summarize existing presentations, identify key slides, and get design assistance in PowerPoint.

Summary

Copilot in Excel can analyze and identify data insights for you in the form of charts, PivotTables, summaries, trends, and outliers. It can transform data by highlighting, sorting, filtering, and formatting it.

It can create column formulas for you and explain how they work, and it can be a research tool and answer questions about your data, something completely different, or even how to accomplish a task in Excel.

In order to be able to use Copilot in Excel, your file must be stored on OneDrive or SharePoint with AutoSave turned on. Using an Excel table is optional, but your active cursor must be in a data range formatted with no empty rows or columns, header rows, and no subtotals.

CHAPTER 7

Copilot in PowerPoint

Somewhere, all over the world, someone is giving a PowerPoint presentation *right now*. At the same time, someone in the world is wondering how to start preparing a PowerPoint presentation they must create and present. It very well could be you!

Not only can Copilot get you started, it can also assist with research and design. It can give you presentation assistance, create slides and add images, and help make sure your presentation is accessible and inclusive in its design.

Like Word and Excel, the Copilot pane in PowerPoint is opened by clicking the Copilot icon in the Home ribbon tab, which should be familiar to you by now. And, once again, I'll begin by telling you the main things the Microsoft AI can help you accomplish in PowerPoint:

1. It can create a presentation based on a prompt, complete with images and speaker notes.

2. It can create a presentation from an existing file or theme, including starting from your organization's brand package template (if your administrator has set this up).

3. It can add slides (including agenda slides), organize your presentation, and add images.

© Jess Stratton 2024
J. Stratton, *Copilot for Microsoft 365*, Inside Copilot,
https://doi.org/10.1007/979-8-8688-0447-2_7

4. It can help you understand, summarize, and identify key points from an existing presentation.

5. It can be a research tool to answer questions, help you learn PowerPoint, and assist with design and presentation tips.

Create a Presentation from a Prompt

To create a presentation based on a prompt, start by opening a new, blank PowerPoint presentation and click the **Copilot** icon on the Home ribbon tab.

Unlike Excel, you do NOT need your presentation to be saved first before you can use Copilot.

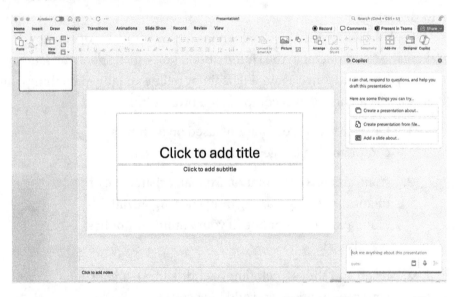

Figure 7-1. *The action buttons at the top of the Copilot pane will get you started when you create a blank presentation*

You can start by clicking the **Create a presentation about...** action button from the top of the Copilot pane. This populates the prompt area at the bottom of the pane and will leave the cursor in position for you to complete the prompt.

Figure 7-2. *Clicking the action button will pre-populate the prompt area, so you can finish the prompt with what your presentation is about*

I'll type the following:

    Create a presentation about community
    outreach for employers.

Figure 7-3. *You can put in as much context as you need to get the presentation content you are looking for*

Depending on the speed of your Internet connection, Copilot will work on the task.

This is a great time to remind you that with all Copilot prompts, you can always click the **Stop generating** button directly under the prompt to immediately stop all processing and return you to the Copilot pane without completing the response.

When finished, you'll have a presentation based on your prompt, complete with topics, images, speaker notes, and a conclusion slide. If you're following along, Copilot will most likely generate different results than what you see in my screenshots. It will choose different content and images even though we may be using the same prompt. This is normal behavior. In fact, if you open PowerPoint tomorrow and type in the same prompt, you'll also notice different results!

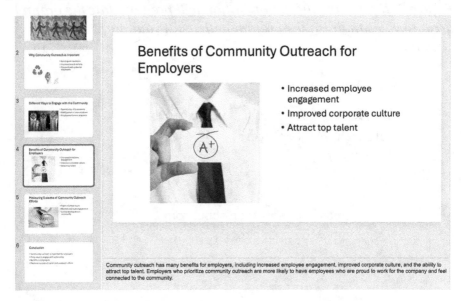

Figure 7-4. *Copilot has even included speaker notes at the bottom of each slide, containing additional talking points on the slide topic. These will be visible to you in Presenter view while presenting, but not visible to the audience*

Just like when we used Copilot to generate text in Word, creating presentations in PowerPoint should be treated as a first-draft basis. This presentation is off to a fantastic start, giving me topic areas I previously hadn't thought of including, but it's nowhere near presentation-ready just yet. As you are *also* familiar by now, you'll see the thumbs-up/thumbs-down icons in the Copilot pane to report back to Microsoft on the quality of Copilot's response.

View More Prompts and Access Copilot Labs

We've used the **View more prompts** icon in both Word and Excel, and in PowerPoint, it works in a similar fashion. You can click this icon to get a list containing four categories to get you started if your prompts need some inspiration. You can click **Create**, **Understand**, **Edit**, and **Ask** to view starting prompts in each category, and click **View more prompts** to open the Copilot Lab dialog box to see a much larger list of things you can ask.

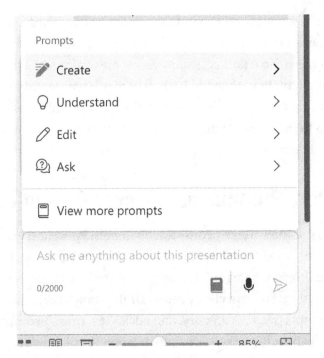

Figure 7-5. *Clicking the View more prompts icon is helpful when you want some ideas about what you can ask Copilot*

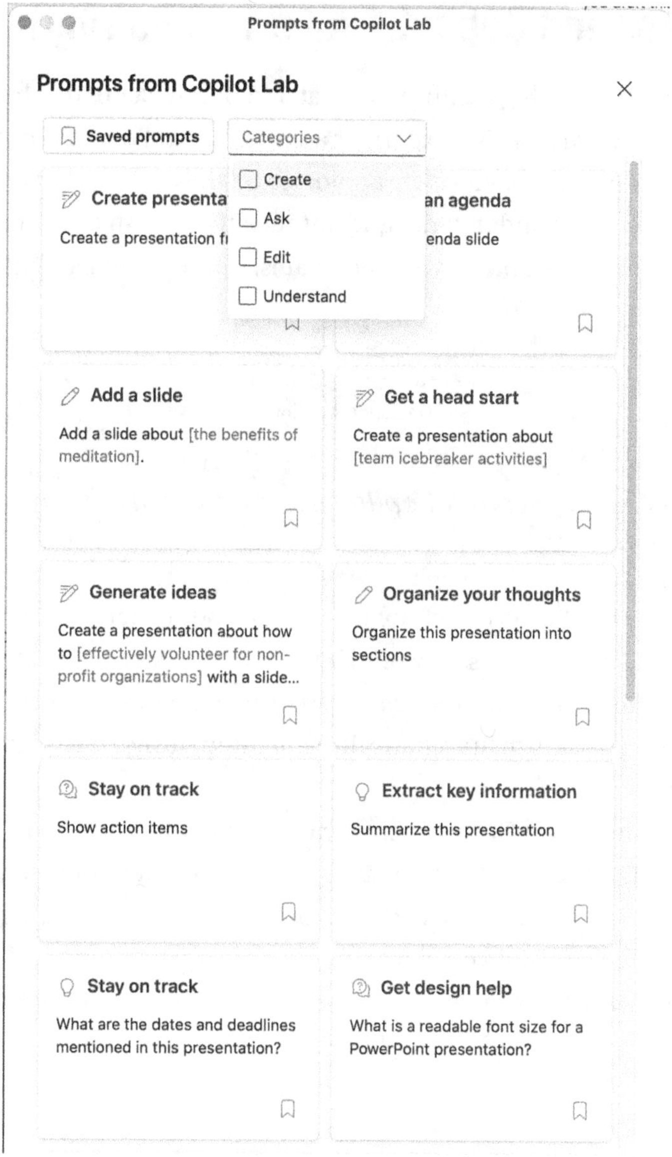

Figure 7-6. *Copilot Lab contains more prompt inspiration*

Designer and Copilot – A Perfect Pairing!

I'm going to make a big assumption that as a purchaser of this book you are most likely *not* a design expert, or a professional PowerPoint slide designer. If you are, you have my apologies on the assumption and will already know, fully understand, and appreciate why I'm about to include a section on the incredible power duo, that is, Copilot and Designer.

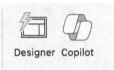

Figure 7-7. *Designer and Copilot are next to each other in the Home ribbon*

Designer is a PowerPoint tool that was introduced in Office 2016 to Microsoft 365 subscribers. Powered by Office Intelligent Services, Designer uses something called *Connected experiences* to analyze your content over the Internet and return automatically generated design ideas for you to choose from.

Both Copilot and Designer are located next to each other on the Home ribbon tab. Once Copilot has created your presentation for you, you can select a slide and modify the text, or change the design. Designer won't modify text for you, but you can certainly make any text edits on your own.

To change the design of a slide, with the slide selected, click the **Designer** icon from the Home ribbon tab.

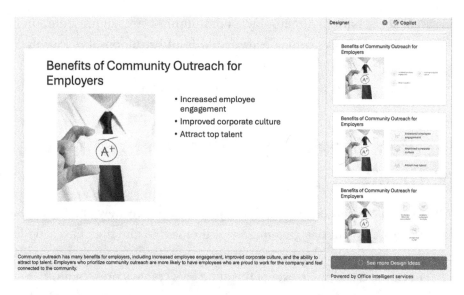

Figure 7-8. *Designer will offer several slide design variations you can choose from. Note the Copilot pane is still open in the tab next to Designer*

Designer will open as a new tabbed pane next to Copilot and will suggest different design options for that slide. You can click on a preferred design to choose it, and it will replace the original slide with the new design.

Make Theme and Color Changes

You can also change to the **Design** tab and choose a new theme or color scheme for your presentation – it's entirely up to you! Once the presentation is in your hands, you can change *any* aspect of it.

Figure 7-9. *Not to be confused with the Designer tool, you can still change to the Design ribbon tab and change the theme or color scheme for your presentation once Copilot has created slides for you*

We'll come back to our employer community outreach presentation in just a moment to make some necessary edits and additions, but I wanted to cover how to use Copilot to create content while using an *existing* presentation, theme, or corporate-branded template.

Create a Presentation from an Existing File or Theme

While you can create a presentation from a completely new blank file, you can also choose your design template or theme first and then have Copilot create content for you around that theme.

The process is similar, except this time let's create a presentation and change to a different theme; in this case, I'll choose a theme called *Madison*. I'll even give my presentation a title: I'm creating a slide deck titled *Presentation Tips for Brand New Speakers*.

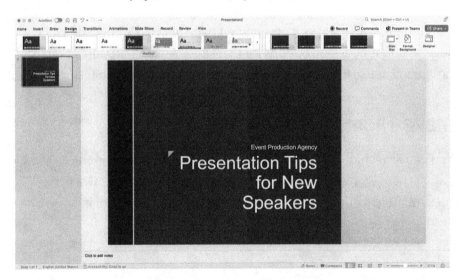

Figure 7-10. *I've created a new presentation, changed the theme, and added content to slides; however, I can still use Copilot with this presentation*

Notice the available layouts based on the theme I chose – this is important when we have Copilot create content for us in a few moments.

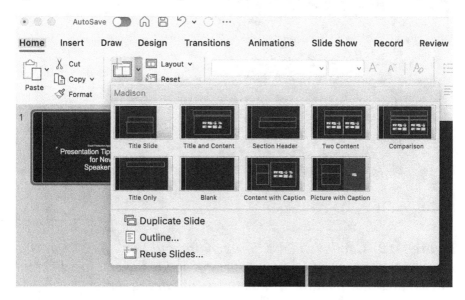

Figure 7-11. *The available layouts change according to the selected theme – Copilot will use these layouts when creating slides*

I can even use a corporate-branded template with Copilot. I might have a particular corporate slide deck already open, or my administrator may have set up an Organizational Asset Library (OAL), in which I could create a new presentation based on one of those templates that will match my existing corporation's brand, colors, and style.

You can prompt Copilot to create a presentation for you while you have the existing file open, and Copilot will design the new presentation *around* the available layouts in your open presentation.

You may notice the top action buttons on the Copilot pane are different when you have an existing file open; we'll go over those later in the chapter.

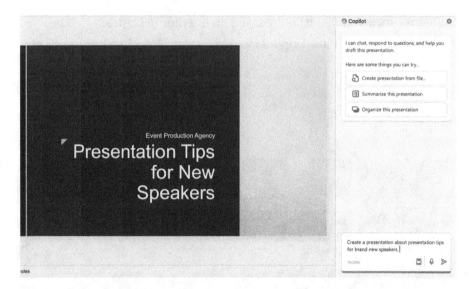

Figure 7-12. *Copilot will use the open presentation's slide layouts to respond to the prompt. Also, note the top action buttons are different when a presentation already has slides containing content*

When Copilot creates your presentation for you, it will overwrite any existing slides you have in your currently open presentation. However, it will pause and give you a chance to save your existing presentation with a different name or location to keep as a backup.

You can click **File ➤ Save As** at this point and give your file a different name before returning to the Copilot pane and clicking the **Create new draft** button to continue creating your presentation.

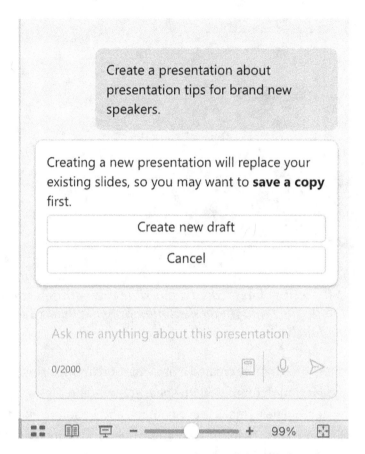

Figure 7-13. *As the presentation already had slides and content, I am prompted to save the presentation first as Copilot will overwrite it with the new content*

In my case, I only have a title slide that I'm not worried about losing, so I'll go ahead and click **Create new draft** without even bothering to save my existing presentation, which is always an option for you.

Figure 7-14. *Copilot has created a ten-slide presentation complete with a new title slide and images, all matching the theme I had selected previously*

Copilot has successfully created a presentation for me using the available slide layouts, complete with speaker notes and topics such as overcoming nervousness, making eye contact, and handling questions.

If I look in the pane, I can see Copilot's response that it has created a ten-slide presentation for me and can help me rewrite slides or use Designer to adjust layouts.

Notice that the word **Designer** is highlighted and boldfaced, and if I hover my mouse over it, the cursor changes to a hand icon. This is a visual cue that I can click directly on the word to access the Designer tool, and clicking will bring up the Designer pane with suggested design changes for the currently selected slide.

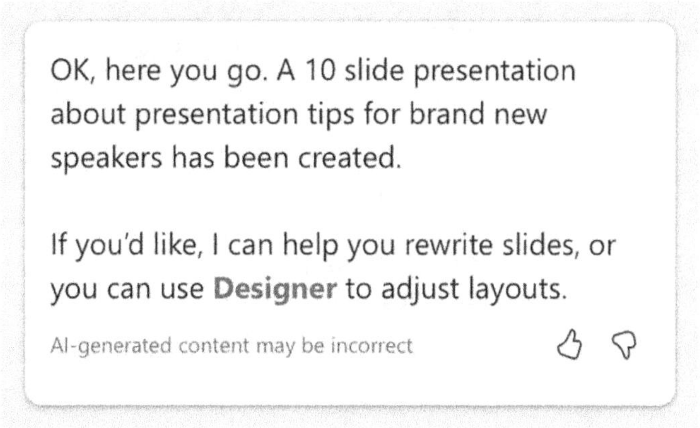

OK, here you go. A 10 slide presentation about presentation tips for brand new speakers has been created.

If you'd like, I can help you rewrite slides, or you can use **Designer** to adjust layouts.

AI-generated content may be incorrect

Figure 7-15. *Note that Designer is highlighted – this is a clickable link to open the Designer tool*

Create a Presentation from a File

You can have Copilot build a presentation around content from an existing Word document. This time, I'm going to create a new blank PowerPoint file, though you could certainly start with a theme or template as we did in the previous exercise. For this exercise, I want to create a presentation around the Employee Handbook I created with Word in Chapter 5.

I'll click the **Create presentation from file** action button, and the prompt area will populate with text. Like Copilot in Word, recent files from OneDrive are suggested after the /, though you can type in the title directly if you know it, as long as it's directly after the forward slash character. You can also include the full URL of the file.

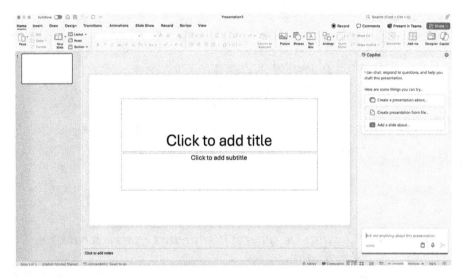

Figure 7-16. *Click the "Create presentation from file" action button to build a presentation from content in a Word document*

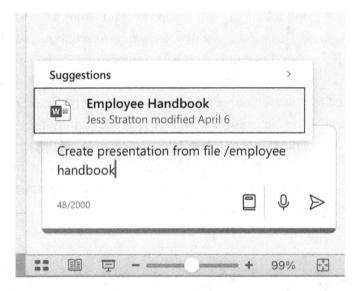

Figure 7-17. *Recent Word documents from OneDrive or Sharepoint will show up as available choices, or you can type a forward slash and a few characters from the document's filename*

The resulting presentation contains eight slides that have been made for me, and while I will certainly be using Designer to adjust the look and feel of all of them, this is a fantastic starting point!

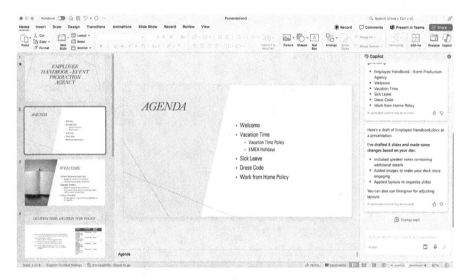

Figure 7-18. *Copilot has created an eight-slide presentation based on the Employee Handbook document we made in Chapter 5*

Add and Organize Slides

I'm going to return to my Community Outreach for Employers presentation. While Copilot created the initial slides, I'd like to add some more and make some changes to the existing slides.

Add an Agenda Slide

Copilot can specifically add an agenda slide for me, giving the audience an overview of each topic in my presentation. In the prompt area, I'll type the following:

        Add an agenda slide.

Copilot will create the slide and again give me the highlighted link to open Designer right from the Copilot pane to refine the design of the new slide.

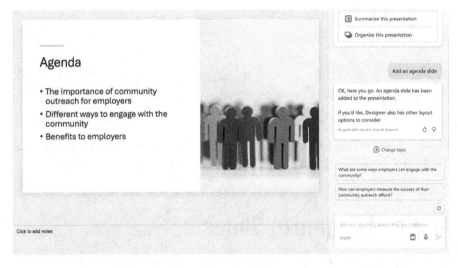

Figure 7-19. *Copilot can add an agenda slide, summarizing the main topics*

Add a New Slide

Reading the agenda, I can see that I'm missing a crucial topic. While I have a topic on the benefits to employers, I'd really like to speak about the benefits to the *employees*.

I'll create the following prompt:

```
Add a slide about the benefits of community
outreach for employees.
```

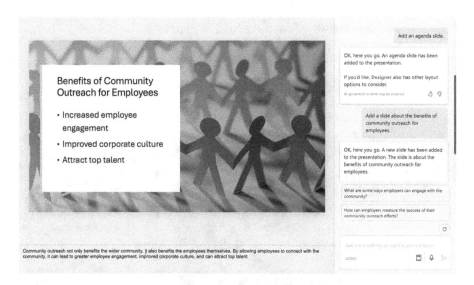

Figure 7-20. *Copilot has created an individual slide with content for me based on my prompt*

The slide is created, and while doing a look-through of the slide deck, I can see some slides that don't have images on them. I'd like to add some to make the content a bit more engaging. Copilot can help!

Add Images

On my conclusion slide, I'll like to add an image. Copilot can add something specific – in our case, I'd like to find a way to visualize community outreach. Perhaps a baseball field, or a garden. However, sometimes you just aren't sure how to properly convey a message through images. As Copilot will add images from the stock library, you can also ask it to add an image about an *idea* to see what it will come up with. As these images come from the stock library, they may or may not be AI generated.

I could try some of the following prompts:

```
Add an image of a baseball field.

Add an image of a garden.

Add an image of community outreach.
```

The last example is an idea, and Copilot has chosen to represent community outreach with a stock photo image of outstretched hands.

Figure 7-21. *Copilot has found an image in the stock library representing an idea*

A quick click on the Designer tab, and I have a fantastic slide to conclude my presentation with.

Figure 7-22. *Copilot created the content and chose the photo, and now the Designer tool assists with the overall slide design*

Add a Slide and an Image at the Same Time

We've been adding a lot of slides where Copilot has created the content. What about when you already have the content you want to add in mind? You can tell Copilot very specifically what you'd like to add, and you can even combine it with an image at the same time. After our conclusion, I'd like to remind our employees that they can contact the HR department if they would like to start a community outreach program within their department.

Let's type the following into the prompt area:

```
Add a slide with the following text: "If you
would like to start a community outreach
program, contact Human Resources to get
started." Include a photo of a smiling
corporate worker.
```

Figure 7-23. *Copilot can create a slide with requested text and imagery at the same time*

In the resulting slide, you can see that while Copilot didn't include the text verbatim, it *did* include everything I asked to create a slide that will only require minimal changes. Excellent!

Organize a Presentation

For this example, I'm going to open my Employee Handbook presentation I made with Copilot earlier. While this example presentation is not long, it's possible I may have a longer presentation that will easily become cumbersome to work with. Not only that, but I may want to change the order in which I talk about each topic.

Copilot can help me organize my presentation by putting each topic into an individual section. Organized sections in PowerPoint makes it easy to drag and drop many slides on the same topic to a new place in your presentation.

I can either click the **Organize this presentation** action button, or I can click **View more prompts ➤ Edit ➤ Organize this presentation**, or I can just type "**Organize this presentation**" directly in the prompt area.

146

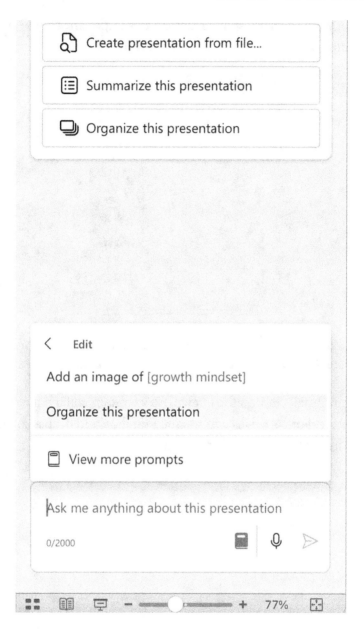

Figure 7-24. *You can use the action buttons or the View more prompt menu to organize your presentation, or type it in directly*

Copilot will return a response that it has grouped my slides into sections and added section title slides for each new section.

Figure 7-25. *Copilot will explain how it sectioned the presentation, and on the left pane, you can see new collapsible labeled sections*

The thumbnail view on the left will now contain collapsible sections. You can expand or collapse each section and drag and drop a collapsed section to a new location in your presentation.

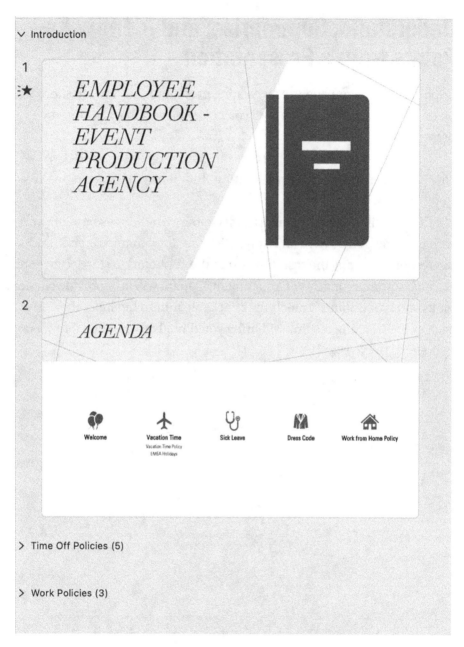

Figure 7-26. *The sections of content can now be moved around easily by dragging and dropping*

Understand, Summarize, and Identify Key Points from a Presentation

Copilot can help you analyze an existing presentation if you are short on time, or just want to make sure you covered everything in your own presentation.

I can summarize an existing presentation by opening it and then choosing **Summarize this presentation** from the action button on the Copilot pane.

Copilot will outline the main points it found in the presentation, and with every response, you can always click the **Copy** button directly under the response to copy the resulting text to the clipboard to store elsewhere.

Like summarizing a Word document, Copilot will also provide citations for its summary points by including clickable numbered links after each point. Clicking the link will bring you directly to the slide that was referenced in the summary.

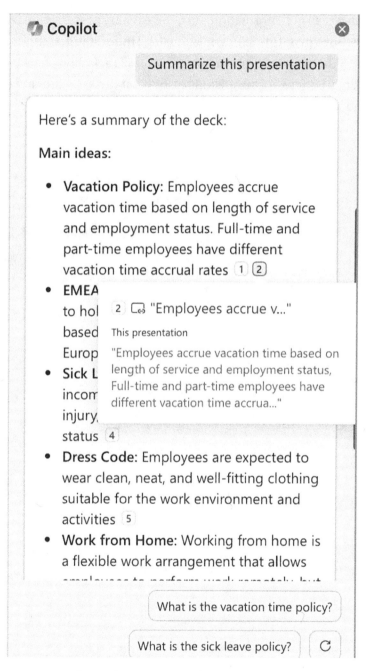

Figure 7-27. Copilot will summarize the slides and provide clickable citations, taking you directly to the slide it is referencing

You can also get information out of an existing presentation by clicking the **View more prompts** icon and choosing **Understand**. Copilot will show you a list of sample questions you can ask including checking for action items, if there are any deadlines, or what the key slides are in the presentation.

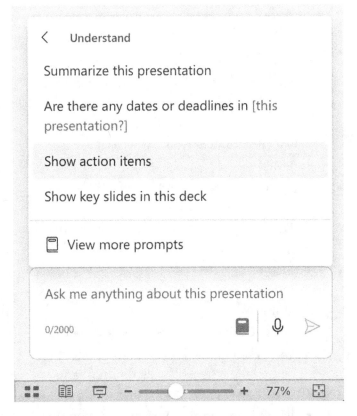

Figure 7-28. *Click "Understand" in the View more prompts area to check for deadlines or action items in the presentation*

Ask, Ask, Ask!

When you summarize a presentation or ask for key points, you are taking the risk that Copilot will correctly return the information that's truly important from the content. You can circumvent all that doubt and chance by directly asking for what information you're looking for in the prompt area.

Directly above the prompt area, Copilot will come up with some specific questions you can ask, and those will change periodically.

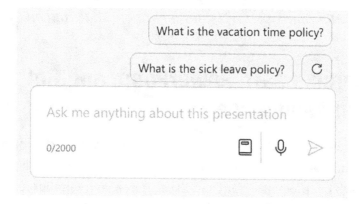

Figure 7-29. *You can click on the specific questions that Copilot suggests above the prompt area, and these will change periodically*

As an employee opening the official Employee Handbook presentation, I might be curious about our holidays. I'll type the following into the prompt area:

Do we get Boxing Day as a holiday?

Copilot gives me a full sentence answer and refers me to the section or slide it got the answer from by providing me with a referenced link so I can verify the information.

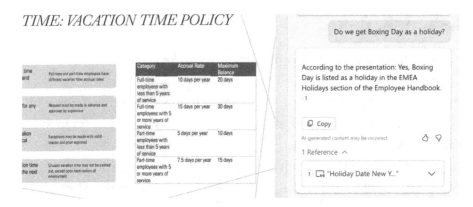

Figure 7-30. *I can ask direct questions about slide content*

Research, Learn PowerPoint, and Get Design Assistance

If you'd prefer not to have Copilot write and create your slides for you, you certainly can still get some help with your own research. Just like I've ended each chapter with Word and Excel, here's your familiar reminder that you can always ask Copilot in PowerPoint *anything*.

In addition, you may need to ask Copilot for help accomplishing tasks in PowerPoint that you can't do by typing a prompt.

As of this publishing, while it *can* add simple animations, Copilot in PowerPoint *cannot* add video or slide transitions.

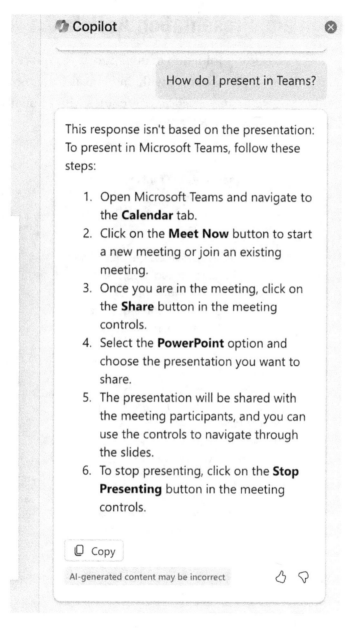

Copilot

How do I present in Teams?

This response isn't based on the presentation: To present in Microsoft Teams, follow these steps:

1. Open Microsoft Teams and navigate to the **Calendar** tab.
2. Click on the **Meet Now** button to start a new meeting or join an existing meeting.
3. Once you are in the meeting, click on the **Share** button in the meeting controls.
4. Select the **PowerPoint** option and choose the presentation you want to share.
5. The presentation will be shared with the meeting participants, and you can use the controls to navigate through the slides.
6. To stop presenting, click on the **Stop Presenting** button in the meeting controls.

Copy

AI-generated content may be incorrect

Figure 7-31. *Copilot can tell you how to accomplish tasks from the Help file*

Get Design and Presentation Assistance

PowerPoint has a unique combination of dual purposes: You're creating slides, which you may need assistance with, but you also are most likely creating them *to present to an audience.* This comes with its own set of challenges that you also may need assistance with.

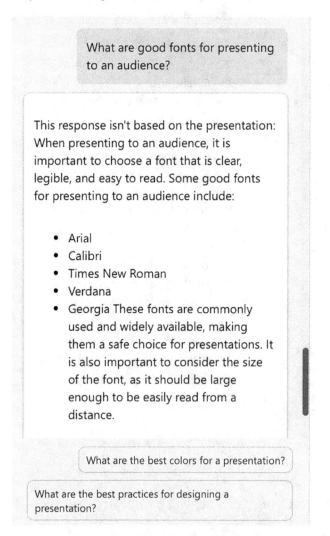

Figure 7-32. *You can ask Copilot for slide design assistance*

You can ask Copilot about font size, color, contrast, and more. You can ask how to make sure your presentation is inclusive and accessible.

> How can I make sure my presentation is inclusive and accessible?

This response isn't based on the presentation: Here are some ways to make sure your presentation is inclusive and accessible:

- Use clear and simple language, avoiding jargon or technical terms that may be difficult for some audience members to understand.
- Use high-contrast colors and large, easy-to-read fonts to ensure that your slides are easy to read.
- Provide alternative text for images, charts, and graphs to ensure that they are accessible to people with visual impairments.
- Use a microphone and ensure that the audio is clear and easy to hear.
- Provide captions or transcripts for any audio or video content.
- Consider the needs of people with mobility impairments and ensure that the presentation venue is accessible.
- Be mindful of cultural differences and avoid using language or imagery that may be offensive or insensitive.

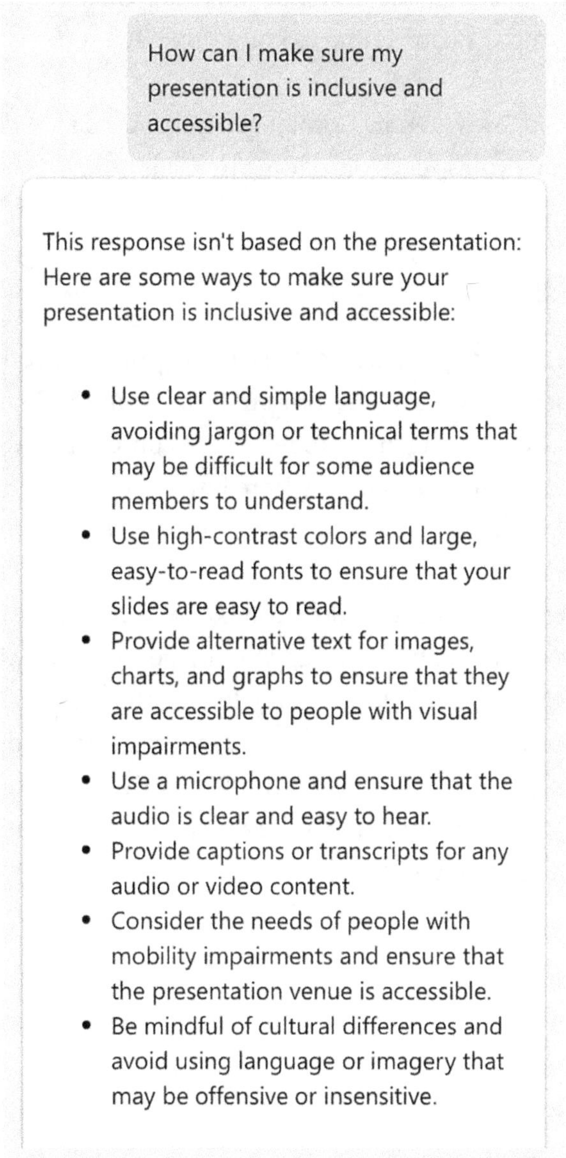

Figure 7-33. *You can ask for presentation tips, design tips, accessibility tips, anything that will help you be the best presenter you can be*

You can ask Copilot for tips and tricks on presenting, rehearsing, and more. So please enjoy, have fun, and good luck on your next presentation you must make in front of an audience (not that you'll need it, of course!). It's never easy, but it's comforting to know you have somewhere to ask all those questions.

Up next, I'll show you how Copilot can help you day to day in an app I already you know you spend lots of time in – Outlook!

Summary

PowerPoint can create presentations based on prompts, complete with images and speaker notes. These presentations should be considered first draft only. While you'll need to refine the content and wording, it's an incredible time-saver, especially if you're having trouble getting started. Once Copilot creates slides for you, you can use Designer to refine the look and feel of the slides.

It can also create a presentation from an existing theme or based on content from an existing file. You can add images to slides with prompts or create slides with specific images you're looking for all in the same prompt.

Finally, it can help you understand, summarize, and identify key points from an existing presentation. You can ask directly, use the action buttons, or view prompts from Copilot Lab to see more ways you can ask Copilot questions about presentations.

CHAPTER 8

Copilot in Outlook

In Word, Excel, and PowerPoint, we've spent a considerable amount of time accessing Copilot from the side pane, and while the Windows version of Outlook does have a side pane, the Mac version does not. Don't worry at all about what version you're using – I'll point out those differences as we go and include images, so you won't miss a thing.

Not only that, but every Outlook-specific prompt that a Windows user can do in the side pane can *also* be done by Mac users later in Chapter 10, so you can be confident that you *really* aren't going to miss a thing.

It's also a good time to remind you that this is focused on what you can accomplish in Outlook if you're a **Copilot for Microsoft 365** user. Copilot Pro users need an *outlook.com, hotmail.com, live.com,* or *msn.com* email address to use Copilot in Outlook and cannot take advantage of chatting with Copilot in the side pane.

Here's what Copilot in Outlook can do for you:

1. It can draft emails and generate content.

2. It can assist with content while replying to emails, including a suggested response.

3. It can summarize an email or conversation thread.

4. It can offer coaching to assist you in tone, clarity, and reader sentiment while writing emails.

J. Stratton, *Copilot for Microsoft 365*, Inside Copilot,
https://doi.org/10.1007/979-8-8688-0447-2_8

5. It can find files and emails and be a research tool *(Windows only in Outlook, Mac users can accomplish this with Microsoft Graph-grounded chat)*.

6. It can help prepare for meetings and answer schedule-related questions *(Windows only in Outlook, Mac users can accomplish this with Microsoft Graph-grounded chat)*.

For Windows users, Copilot for Microsoft 365 is available in both classic and the latest version of Outlook, also called the *new* Outlook. For Mac users, Copilot for Microsoft 365 in Outlook is *only* available with new Outlook. The new Outlook contains additional features and a slightly different user interface.

You can enable this new user interface by clicking the toggle button labeled **Try the new Outlook** at the top right-hand side of the screen.

On a Mac, the toggle button is labeled **Legacy Outlook** and you won't see it at all if you're already using the new Outlook.

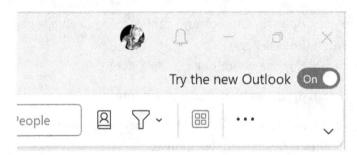

Figure 8-1. *Toggle the new Outlook on to use Copilot in Outlook (labeled Legacy Outlook if you're on a Mac)*

Windows users can verify you're using the new Outlook by the toggle button labeled **New Outlook** as shown in Figure 8-2. Note the Copilot icon directly above it!

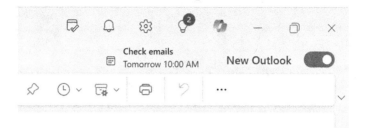

Figure 8-2. The Copilot icon is directly above the New Outlook toggle, letting you know that you're able to use Copilot successfully. Mac users won't see the toggle anymore

Draft Emails and Generate Content

Copilot in Outlook can help you draft the content of an email. Perhaps you're struggling with how to start, unsure of how to address a sensitive topic, or maybe you're just pressed for time. Whatever the reason is, Copilot can get you started with that first draft.

Click the **New mail** button to compose an email. Here's where the Mac and Windows versions differ again.

Windows

Windows users can initiate Copilot by clicking the icon that appears on the Message ribbon tab and choosing **Draft with Copilot**.

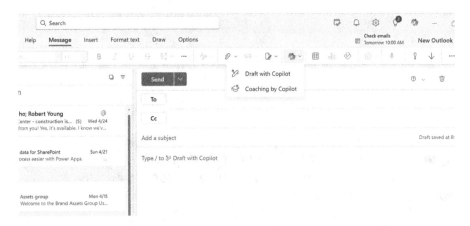

Figure 8-3. *Click Draft with Copilot in the Message ribbon tab*

Alternatively, you can bring up the dialog box by placing the cursor in the body of the email and hitting the / key. The **Draft with Copilot** button appears at the top of the list, along with recently modified files you may want to include as an attachment.

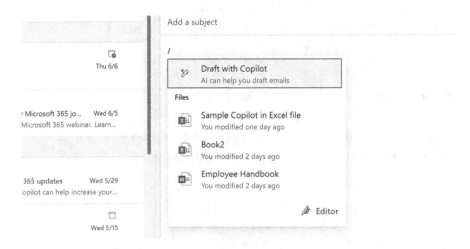

Figure 8-4. *After typing a forward slash, click Draft with Copilot to generate text*

Mac

On a Mac, the Draft with Copilot button can be found on the message formatting toolbar, right above the message body.

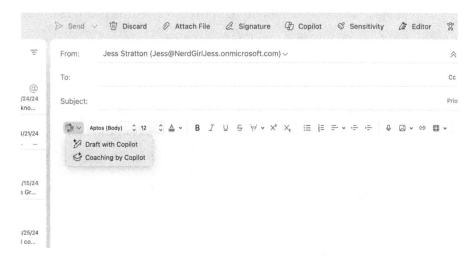

Figure 8-5. *On a Mac, the Draft with Copilot button is found on the toolbar in the message body*

Using the Draft with Copilot Dialog Box

Type your prompt into the dialog box, giving as much or as little context as you feel you need to provide to get a good response. I'll type the following:

> Act as a manager. Write an email to the team
> requesting a list of speakers for their next
> event, any due dates for presentations,
> and any roadblocks they are encountering.
> Let them know to be on the lookout for a
> calendar invitation for an all-team meeting
> next week and to have a brief overview of
> their progress ready to discuss.

Clicking the two horizontal lines at the bottom of the prompt window allows you to further refine the tone and length of the response. Do you want a shorter, or longer email? Do you want the overall tone to be direct, or more casual?

I'll change mine to be of medium length instead of the default choice of short, but I'll keep the tone as direct.

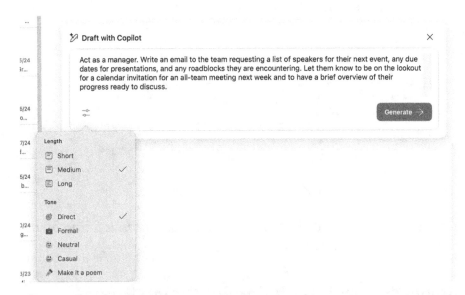

Figure 8-6. *The Windows version has the same functionality without the icons next to the text*

After reading the draft response, you can use the thumbs-up/down buttons, or choose to refine the response or keep it. You can provide additional context, or perhaps fix an error.

I did ask Copilot to write an email to my entire team, but as I read the response, the opening line is as follows: *"I hope this email finds you well."* Copilot seems to think the email is only being sent to an individual, not a group. I'm going to type the following as a refinement:

```
Write the email to the entire team instead
of as if I'm only talking to one person.
```

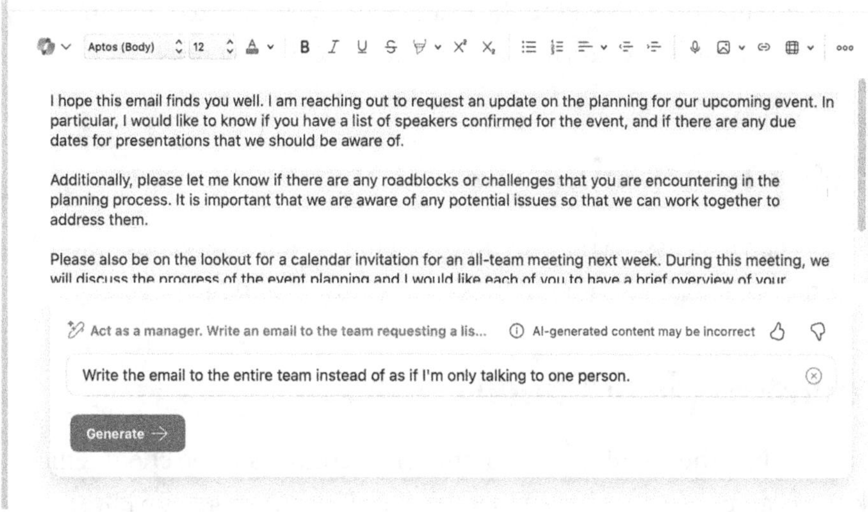

I hope this email finds you well. I am reaching out to request an update on the planning for our upcoming event. In particular, I would like to know if you have a list of speakers confirmed for the event, and if there are any due dates for presentations that we should be aware of.

Additionally, please let me know if there are any roadblocks or challenges that you are encountering in the planning process. It is important that we are aware of any potential issues so that we can work together to address them.

Please also be on the lookout for a calendar invitation for an all-team meeting next week. During this meeting, we will discuss the progress of the event planning and I would like each of you to have a brief overview of your

✏ Act as a manager. Write an email to the team requesting a lis...   ⓘ AI-generated content may be incorrect   👍   👎

Write the email to the entire team instead of as if I'm only talking to one person.   ⊗

Generate →

Figure 8-7. *I can refine the response, which will change and clarify the text*

The resulting response is much better, containing phrasing that includes everyone. I still can go back and use the first draft at any time. Just like when we refined a response in Word, I can use the arrows at the top to go back and forth between drafts.

I can click the big blue button labeled **Keep It** if I'm happy with that draft or **Discard** to start over. I can always click **Regenerate** to create a new draft with my refinements.

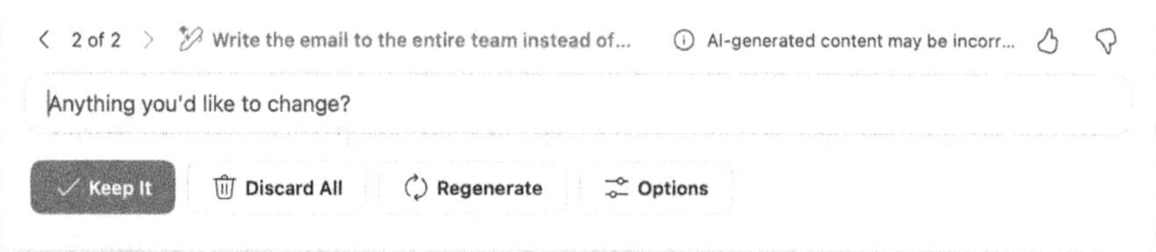

<   2 of 2   >   ✏ Write the email to the entire team instead of...   ⓘ AI-generated content may be incorr...   👍   👎

Anything you'd like to change?

✓ Keep It   🗑 Discard All   ⟳ Regenerate   ⚊ Options

Figure 8-8. *The arrows on the top left will take me through each generated draft*

Once you choose **Keep It**, the draft response is inserted into the body of the email, and it's yours to make any additional changes.

Reply to Emails

Copilot can also assist you with drafting email replies. As with composing, the process is slightly different between Windows and Mac.

Windows *(New Outlook Only)*

After reading the email, the top of the email contains three choices that Copilot can use to draft a response for you. These responses will vary depending on the content of the email.

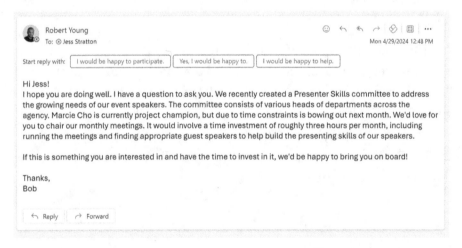

Figure 8-9. *Three choices appear at the top to generate reply text*

These options are generally available to you the first time the email is opened – if you return to the email later, you may notice that the response options are no longer there, though it's not unheard of to see them again.

I've found that sometimes I can mark the email as unread to get them to return; otherwise, this is where the steps for both Windows *and* Mac converge to use Copilot for replying.

Using the Reply with Copilot Dialog Box

Copilot can give you a different set of responses that you can choose from based on the context of the email.

Mac

On a Mac, click the Copilot icon to the left of the reply to buttons and choose **Reply with Copilot**.

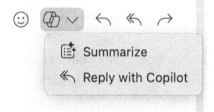

Figure 8-10. On Mac, click the Copilot icon next to the reply to buttons and choose Reply with Copilot

The dialog box is like the *Draft with Copilot* box with one difference – there are three context-related choices I can use as prompts. I can absolutely ignore these options and put in my own reply. There's no right or wrong choice here; it's whatever works best for you in each situation.

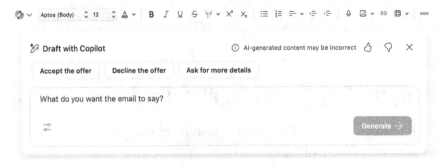

Figure 8-11. *The email is a request to chair a committee; Copilot has offered me some canned prompts to generate a reply, such as accepting or declining the offer*

Windows

Windows does not have the Copilot icon next to the reply to buttons, so you'll have to click **Reply** to get started. At the very bottom of the screen, you'll see the **Draft with Copilot** area. Notice the reply options are remarkably like those on the Mac!

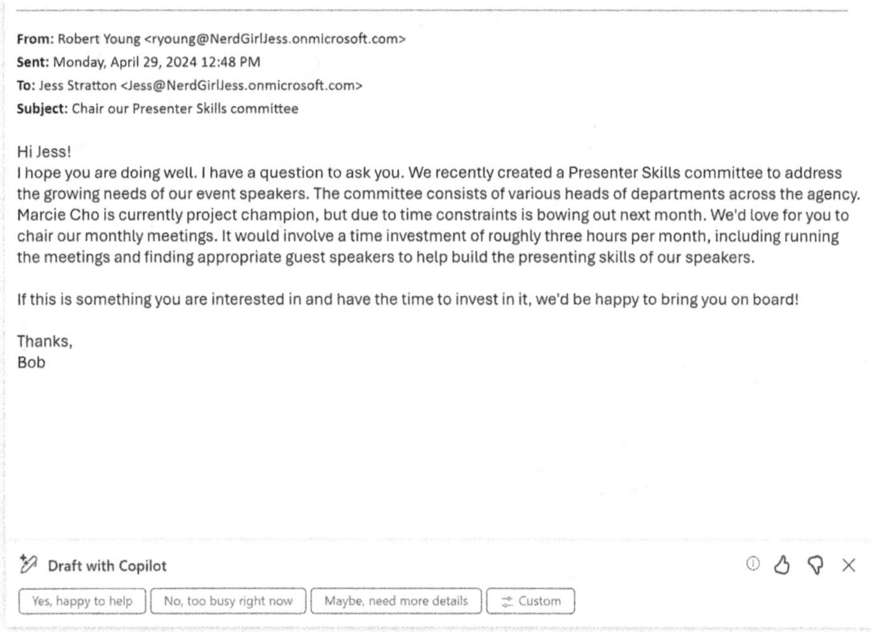

From: Robert Young <ryoung@NerdGirlJess.onmicrosoft.com>

Sent: Monday, April 29, 2024 12:48 PM

To: Jess Stratton <Jess@NerdGirlJess.onmicrosoft.com>

Subject: Chair our Presenter Skills committee

Hi Jess!

I hope you are doing well. I have a question to ask you. We recently created a Presenter Skills committee to address the growing needs of our event speakers. The committee consists of various heads of departments across the agency. Marcie Cho is currently project champion, but due to time constraints is bowing out next month. We'd love for you to chair our monthly meetings. It would involve a time investment of roughly three hours per month, including running the meetings and finding appropriate guest speakers to help build the presenting skills of our speakers.

If this is something you are interested in and have the time to invest in it, we'd be happy to bring you on board!

Thanks,
Bob

✏️ Draft with Copilot   ⓘ 🔥 ▽ ✕

| Yes, happy to help | No, too busy right now | Maybe, need more details | ⇌ Custom |

Figure 8-12. *In Windows, the Copilot reply prompts are at the bottom of the email*

Alternatively (and for classic Outlook users), you can access the **Draft with Copilot** dialog and options by clicking the Copilot icon which appears on the Message ribbon tab when the cursor is placed in the body of the reply.

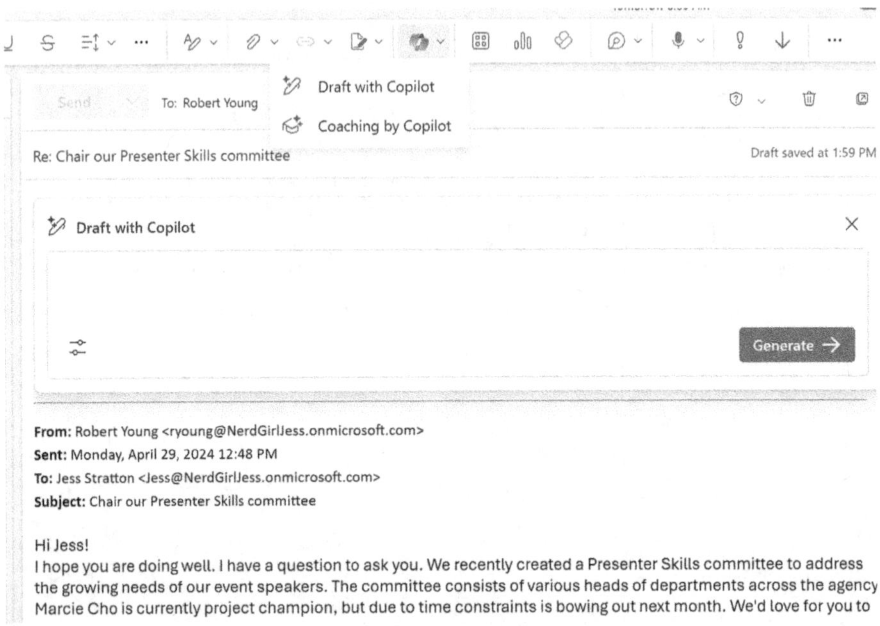

Figure 8-13. *You do not have to use Copilot's context replies; you can always create your own draft in a reply*

You'll just have to type your own prompt. Remember, it can be as simple as "Sorry, I'm too busy right now," and you can change the tone and length to match your sentiment. You aren't just adding that one line of text; you're using that line of text as a prompt to generate a larger, more fleshed out response.

Summarize an Email or Conversation Thread

One of the first things you may have noticed about Copilot in Outlook is the **Summary by Copilot** area at the top of *every* email, and that includes entire conversations of replies.

Clicking the **Summary by Copilot** button will allow Copilot to scan the email or conversation for key topics it will return.

Let's take Figure 8-14 as an example; this looks like a lengthy email thread! Rather than scrolling through it all, let's have Copilot summarize it.

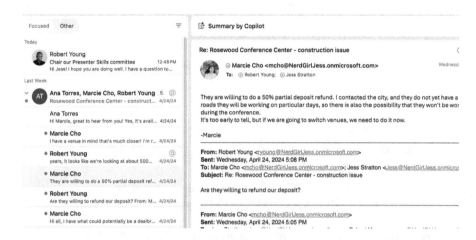

Figure 8-14. *Copilot can summarize this lengthy conversation thread for me by clicking the Summary by Copilot button at the top of the email*

I'll start by clicking on the latest email in the thread, and then I'll click **Summary by Copilot** at the very top of the email.

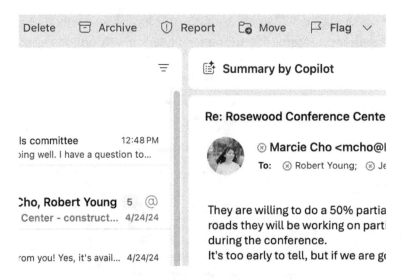

Figure 8-15. *A close-up of the Summary by Copilot button*

Copilot will return a tidy summary at the top of the email, complete with citations that I can click on to go directly to the email.

Figure 8-16. *The summary contains clickable citations*

Summaries aren't just for email conversation threads to explain a lengthy back-and-forth discussion. You can summarize *any* email, including a singular one that's particularly long, or one you're afraid of missing a key point or action item.

Get Coaching Assistance on Tone, Clarity, and Reader Sentiment

Copilot can also assist you in writing your *own* emails before you hit send. Maybe you want to improve your writing skills, make sure you're conveying the right message, or don't want to possibly offend or confuse the reader. Whatever the reason, you can use the **Coaching by Copilot** tool to gain insight and check for tone, clarity, and reader sentiment on your writing.

To get started, begin by composing your email. For this example, we'll use the following text:

> Hello Ms. Torres,
>
> My company Solace Productions holds conventions and conferences in which we gather top industry professionals to speak to an audience on a chosen topic.
>
> Many of our speakers do not have formal presentation skills, and that is where I would love your assistance. Would you be interested in giving a webinar on presentation skills for our first-time speakers? We offer competitive payment for speakers, and it would be very beneficial to our speakers.
>
> I look forward to hearing from you!
>
> Sincerely,
>
> Jess

Windows

To invoke Coaching by Copilot on Outlook in Windows, compose your email and click the Copilot icon on the Message ribbon tab. From there, choose **Coaching by Copilot**.

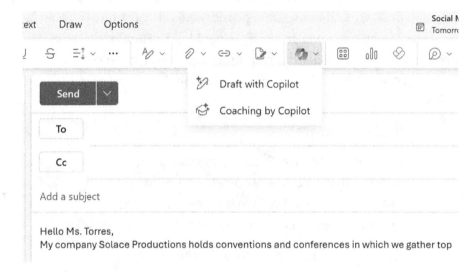

Figure 8-17. *On Windows, the Copilot icon is on the Message ribbon tab*

Mac

On a Mac, compose your email and click the Copilot button on the message formatting toolbar. From there, choose **Coaching by Copilot**.

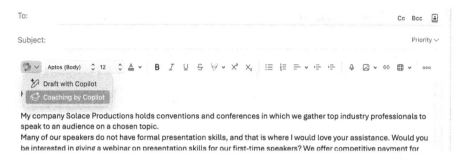

Figure 8-18. *On a Mac, the Copilot icon is in the message body formatting toolbar*

Copilot will return three categories of coaching: tone, reader sentiment, and clarity.

Tone

Copilot will return advice on how you can adjust your email to make sure you're sending across the right *tone*. For example, could you be more confident? More polite? Less pushy? It will give you practical examples of how you can reword your existing text.

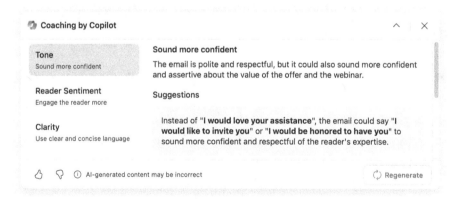

Figure 8-19. *Copilot thinks I should sound more confident in my email and gives me alternate phrasing to help*

Reader Sentiment

How will the reader react to your message? What emotions or feelings will it invoke? How will it make them *feel*? Copilot can give you an idea of how your message may be received by the recipient in a tab called *reader sentiment.*

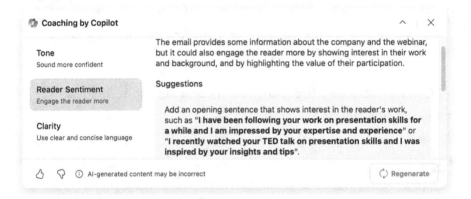

Figure 8-20. *Copilot thinks I should show the recipient the true value they will add*

In our example, Copilot lets me know that I could engage the reader more by highlighting the value of their participation by including some examples of their existing work.

Clarity

The final piece of advice Coaching by Copilot can give me is on the *clarity* of my message. How concise is the text? Am I using passive or active voice? Is the text confusing, or too wordy?

Figure 8-21. *Copilot can help my writing become more precise*

Over time, coaching can help you become much more efficient at business communication (a fine and valuable skill!). However, remember that you don't *have* to use the coaching advice. You can close out of the dialog entirely and forget you ever read it, or you can always click **Regenerate** to get some more coaching tips. Even the most confident writer has vulnerable moments, and it's nice to know the tool is there for you when and if you need it.

Find Files and Answer Questions About Email *(Windows Only in New Outlook)*

Copilot in Outlook can draft emails for you, create replies, summarize emails, and even give you valuable coaching on your writing. The Windows version of new Outlook has *one* additional tool, and that's the Copilot pane on the right-hand side that we've been using throughout this book.

It's important to note that any email and calendar prompts I use as examples in this section can all be used on a Mac in Microsoft Graph-grounded chat, which I'll be covering in Chapter 10.

To open the pane in Outlook on Windows, click the **Copilot** icon on the top right-hand side of the screen.

Figure 8-22. *The Copilot icon at the top of the screen in Outlook for Windows*

You'll see an arrangement you are familiar with: the prompt area on the bottom and some action buttons to get you started on top.

New Outlook

Ɔ ⌄ ⬦ ...

⬈ | ⬦ | ⊞ | ...

Mon 4/29/2024 12:48 PM

Copilot   ✕

💡 **Understand**

Tell me more about [topic]

🔍 **Find something**

Find the file that [person shared last week about]

▤ **Stay on top**

Summarize recent emails where I was @mentioned

y created a
vent speakers. The
igency. Marcie Cho
ng out next month.
ı time investment of
d finding
ur speakers.

st in it, we'd be

Try using one of the prompts above

0/2000   ▷

Figure 8-23. *The Copilot pane in Outlook for Windows has action buttons on top and the prompt area at the bottom*

As usual, you can use this as a research tool, but now you can also ask questions about your email. Are you looking for a particular attachment? What have you and a particular coworker been talking about recently? Do you need a summary of all the emails you were @mentioned in last week?

I won't go into too many examples here. I want to save them all for Chapter 10.

Finally, I'm going to head over to the calendar area of Outlook, which is one last area where the Copilot pane can answer questions for you. Again, this is for Windows only.

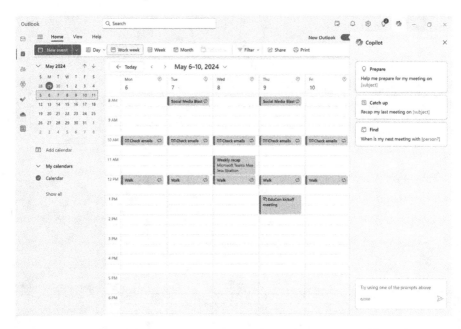

Figure 8-24. *The Copilot pane's action buttons are all calendar and meeting related*

Notice how the questions are related to my calendar and meetings. Here, I can ask Copilot when my next meeting is with a particular person. I can ask for a list of when all my EduCon meetings are. I can ask for meeting recaps from Teams, and you'll also see this in action in the next chapter.

Because of this, I'm going to save the rest of the examples for the remaining chapters. In the meantime, you can get to know the software better by *playing around*. Ask Copilot lots of questions about your important emails, correspondence, schedule, and attachments in Outlook. Think of how you like to get organized, or what you could ask Copilot about your schedule to help prepare you at the start of your work week. How could it help you at the *end* of your work week?

Everything that you can ask here, you can also ask in the next chapter. It's all thanks to Microsoft Graph-grounded chat, and I'll talk about it next in Teams!

Summary

Copilot in Outlook is available in both classic and new Outlook for Windows and only in the new Outlook for Mac. Copilot can draft emails, generate content, and assist with content while replying to emails. In fact, it includes several suggested responses you can choose from to base a generated reply from.

If you prefer to write your own emails, it can offer coaching to assist you in tone, clarity, and reader sentiment.

In Windows, it can find files and emails, help prepare for meetings, and answer schedule-related questions. For both Windows and Mac users, this can also be accomplished with Microsoft Graph-grounded chat, which I'll be covering in depth in Chapter 10.

CHAPTER 9

Copilot in Teams

Microsoft Teams is your one-stop shop for collaboration. You can hold video meetings, chat as a group or individual, share files, and view your schedule. You can even use Microsoft Graph-grounded chat directly within Teams for even greater productivity.

Teams is fantastic for firing off quick questions to coworkers without needing email. Your chat history is saved, along with dedicated tabs to easily view shared files from your conversations. Now with Copilot, there's no need to search or endlessly scroll to find the answer to a question from an old chat; you can summarize group or individual chat threads or ask specific questions about the content. In fact, you can do a lot more.

Here's what Copilot can do in Microsoft Teams:

1. It can catch you up and answer questions while you're in a meeting.

2. It can recap and answer questions about past meetings.

3. It can summarize and answer questions about group or individual chat threads.

4. It can rewrite a message for better tone and clarity before sending.

5. It can use Microsoft Graph-grounded chat to answer questions about your organization.

© Jess Stratton 2024
J. Stratton, *Copilot for Microsoft 365*, Inside Copilot,
https://doi.org/10.1007/979-8-8688-0447-2_9

Catch Up During Live Meetings

Copilot's ability to assist while meetings are occurring is becoming one of the AI's most prominent features and selling point. While a meeting is going on, you can catch up what you might have missed, summarize key points or action items, find out what issues are still unresolved, and generate meeting notes.

Once the meeting is over, Copilot will be available to answer questions about the meeting in the **Recap** tab, which I'll talk about later.

To use Copilot during and after a meeting, there is one major prerequisite that must be in place: The meeting *must* be transcribed to be able to use Copilot during a meeting. If your subject matter is confidential and you do not want to retain the transcription once the meeting ends, you can still use Copilot during the meeting to answer questions. Copilot does have the ability to use a temporary transcription just for use during the meeting. I'll come back to that in a moment.

For this next example, I am going to be a few minutes late to a meeting. I've asked my manager Marcie Cho to record and transcript the meeting.

To accomplish this, when Marcie starts the meeting, she will click the three dots labeled **More**, hover her mouse over **Record and transcribe**, and choose **Start recording**.

I do want to point out here that recording is not a prerequisite to use Copilot during meetings, only transcription. If you do not wish to record the meeting, you can only choose **Start transcription** instead.

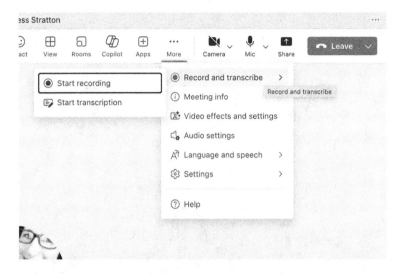

Figure 9-1. *The meeting must be transcribed to use Copilot to recap the meeting, though you can record AND transcribe it*

When I finally join the meeting, if the meeting has been going on for at least five minutes, I'll get a pop-up dialog asking if I want to open Copilot and recap the meeting. I can click **Open Copilot** to accomplish this.

Figure 9-2. *Copilot will ask if you want to see what you missed when you join a meeting at least five minutes after it started*

If you don't see the pop-up, or it's been less than five minutes since the meeting has started, you can click the Copilot icon at any time in the Teams menu bar to open the right-side Copilot pane. From there, you can ask for a recap in multiple ways, whichever feels the most natural to you:

Catch me up.

What did I miss?

Recap the meeting so far.

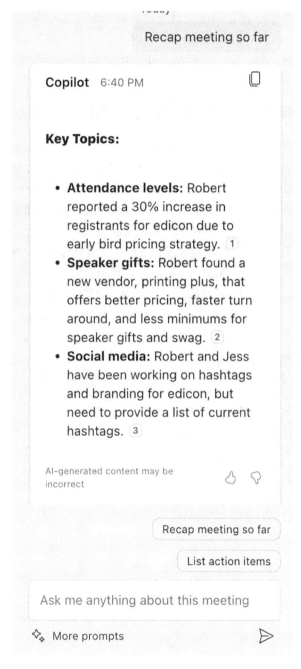

Figure 9-3. *Copilot can recap what you missed when you arrive late to a meeting*

Copilot will give you a summary of who said what, including citations that will bring you to the transcription of the meeting. This is also useful when you need to step away from a meeting for a few minutes.

Get Action Items and Questions Answered

Not only can Copilot summarize a meeting while it's going on, but it can also answer questions and detect actionable items spoken by meeting participants. While the meeting is running, you can use Copilot as your personal assistant in the sidebar pane. I'll mention this later in the chapter to remind you, but unlike the Chat pane during a meeting that's available to everyone, no one in the meeting can see your Copilot pane – it's just for you.

You can ask Copilot where your teammates agree or disagree on a topic. You can ask Copilot to come up with some follow-up questions for a certain team member. You can ask for facts and figures that were mentioned in the meeting.

Try the following prompts in your next meeting with Copilot:

Put all the action items into a table.

Create bullet points of action items.

Generate meeting notes.

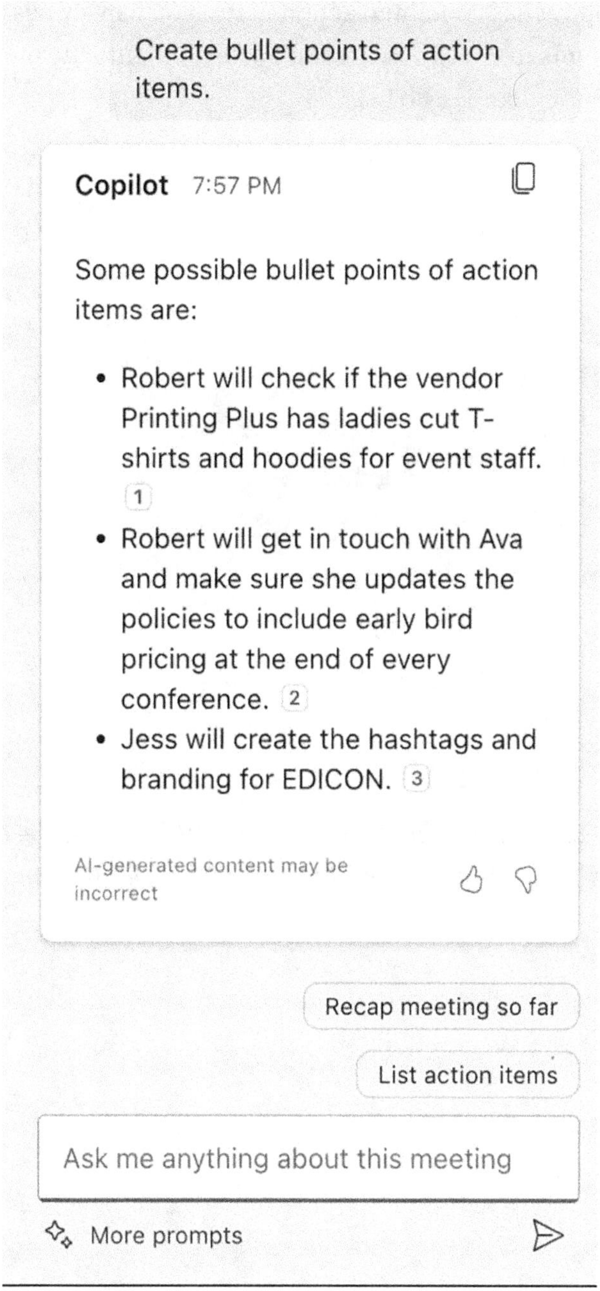

Create bullet points of action items.

Copilot 7:57 PM

Some possible bullet points of action items are:

- Robert will check if the vendor Printing Plus has ladies cut T-shirts and hoodies for event staff. [1]
- Robert will get in touch with Ava and make sure she updates the policies to include early bird pricing at the end of every conference. [2]
- Jess will create the hashtags and branding for EDICON. [3]

AI-generated content may be incorrect

Recap meeting so far

List action items

Ask me anything about this meeting

More prompts

Figure 9-4. *Copilot can create bullet points of actionable items*

Once Copilot has generated action items, you can always click the icon to copy the items to the clipboard and paste them into the meeting chat for your other team members to use.

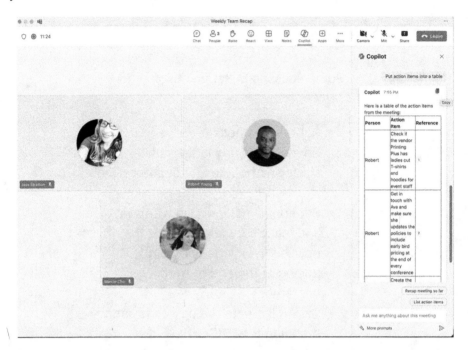

Figure 9-5. *Actionable items have been put into a table, and I can click the Copy button to paste into the meeting chat*

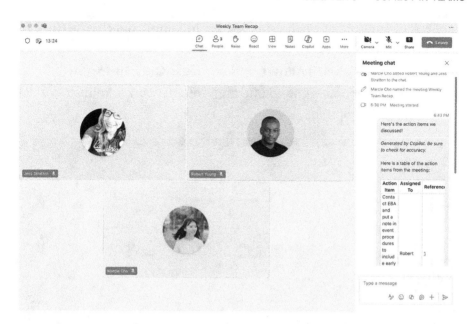

Figure 9-6. *Note I'm in the meeting chat instead of the Copilot pane;*
I can paste in the action items for the meeting participants even if they
don't use Copilot

Once the meeting's scheduled end time is approaching, you'll be
notified via Copilot. This is a great time to get a summary of key points or
send out action items to participants.

Use Copilot Without Saving a Recording
or Transcription

You may wish to use Copilot during a meeting, but not retain the recording
or transcription after. This is useful in situations where the subject matter
is sensitive or confidential, yet Copilot can still assist with answering
questions, summarizing key points, and creating action items while the
meeting is in progress.

To accomplish this, open your meeting in Teams, and choose **Options** and then **More options**.

In the section labeled **Allow Copilot**, choose **Only during the meeting**. If this option is grayed out, then your network administrator has not given you this option.

Figure 9-7. *The network administrator has given the meeting owner permission to choose whether Copilot can be used after the meeting is over to answer questions*

Recap Past Meetings

Once your meetings have ended, you can still use Copilot to ask questions and get reminded of actionable items. Both Teams Premium and Copilot for Microsoft 365 contain a special feature called *Intelligent recap*, an AI-assisted comprehensive overview of your meeting.

You can find Intelligent recap by going to your meeting and choosing the **Recap** tab at the top.

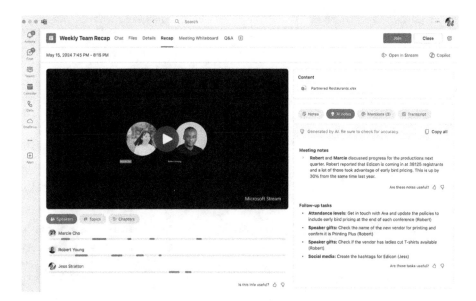

Figure 9-8. *Intelligent recap allows you to get AI-assisted summaries of past meetings*

You'll see the speakers from your meeting and when they spoke. You'll see your meeting laid out and organized by chapter so you can quickly jump from topic to topic. You can see where you were @mentioned in the chat, the transcription of the meeting, and any attached files. You'll see meeting notes followed up by a tidy list of follow-up tasks in the tab labeled **AI notes**.

Here's where Copilot differs from Teams Premium. Copilot for Microsoft 365 subscribers can click the Copilot icon on the top right-hand side while in the recap area to open the traditional sidebar pane and continue to ask questions about your meeting. It's important to note that if given the option, the meeting organizer must have set the option to use Copilot during *and* after the meeting. Also, if the recording and/or transcription was not started until later in the meeting, Copilot can only answer questions after those features were turned on.

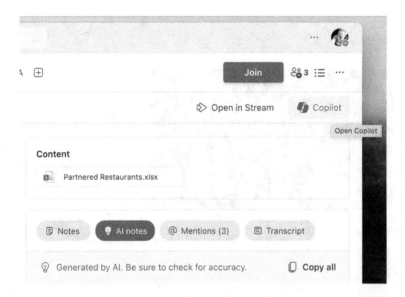

Figure 9-9. *The Copilot button can still be used after the meeting is over to answer questions*

When you open the pane, you'll see any chats you already had asked Copilot while the meeting was occurring. You can continue the chat or ask a new question.

Summarize Group or Individual Chat Threads

Aside from meetings, Teams is incredibly useful for firing off a quick question to a teammate, or multiple members of your team. Those chats can get long, and finding what you're looking for can involve a *lot* of time-wasting scrolling. Fortunately, Copilot can also assist in answering questions in your chat threads.

To get started, click **Chat** on the leftmost navigation bar, and open the specific thread you want to ask Copilot questions about.

You'll see the Copilot icon on the top right-hand side of the thread. The pane will open, and you'll be able to ask questions about that *specific* group or individual chat thread.

Figure 9-10. *Open your chat and click the Copilot icon on the top left-hand side to open the Copilot pane and ask questions about that chat thread*

A slight difference here versus other Copilot panes we've seen is that the text at the top of the pane contains helpful *reminders* for you, not action buttons, as shown in Figure 9-11.

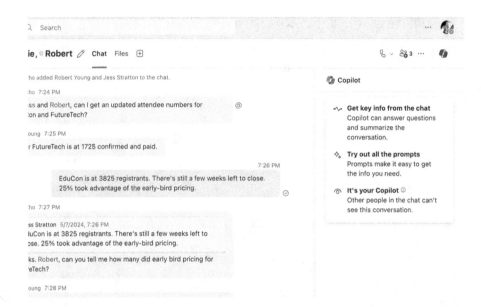

Figure 9-11. *You'll be reminded that it's your Copilot – other people in the chat won't be able to see your conversations with Copilot*

It's *Your* Copilot

There's an important reminder listed in the pane that I want to mention, and it's labeled **It's your Copilot**. I mentioned this earlier in the chapter, and it's important enough to revisit. It's there to remind you that the other participants in the chat do *not* see the conversations you're having with Copilot, unlike in a Teams meeting where the chat window is available for everyone to use together. Why is this so important? I don't want you to feel vulnerable about using the tool. It might make you afraid to ask questions and I don't want that! Did you forget a key detail or an important due date? Ask Copilot about it. Your teammates won't know.

While your teammates won't know, your administrator *may* be able to see your Copilot chat history. This will be unique to everyone's organization based on how it was set up and it's an important enough fact to mention here. However, I still don't want you to be afraid to ask Copilot questions that will make your workday more productive. Is your network administrator worried that you need a reminder about an important due date? Probably not.

I can see a long chat between myself, Robert, and Marcie Cho. I need to know how many people are attending a popular conference called EduCon so I know how many programs to print, and I also know that we've talked about it *somewhere* in the chat. I'll ask Copilot a direct question about it:

How many registrants does EduCon have?

Not only does Copilot give me the answer but will also cite the source, giving me a numbered link to go directly to the chat entry it got the answer from so I can double-check Copilot's response.

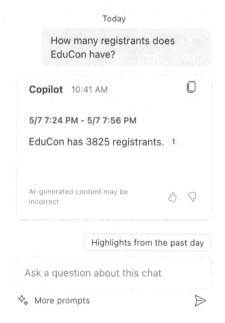

Figure 9-12. *Copilot will cite the answers it gives with clickable links to your Teams chats*

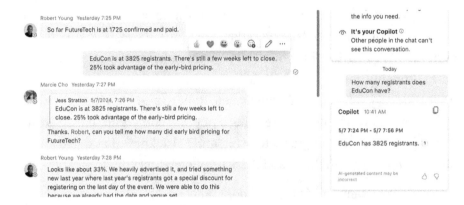

Figure 9-13. *Clicking the citation takes me directly to the chat line Copilot got its answer from*

A particularly active chat can be difficult to keep up with, especially if you're coming back to Teams after being away for a while. For that reason, Copilot has the fantastic ability to be able to highlight key topics from the past day, week, or month.

At the bottom of the Copilot pane, click **More prompts**. From there, choose your highlight choice, or some of the other prompt suggestions that may be included and useful to you. I'll choose to view highlights from the past seven days.

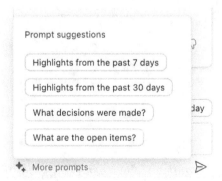

Figure 9-14. *Copilot can give you highlights of conversations to help you catch up on missed chats*

Copilot shows me the specific date range it's highlighting the key information from. It tells me who said what and when and gave me a bulleted list of key takeaways, complete with clickable citations. Thanks, Copilot!

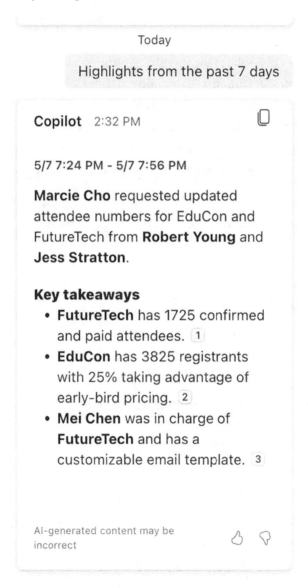

Figure 9-15. *Highlights contain bullet points and a list of who said what*

Rewrite Messages for Better Tone and Clarity

Even though Teams is made for quick communication between teammates, that doesn't have to mean *poor* communication, nor does it mean you can't be looking for ways to communicate more effectively. I showed you back in Chapter 5 how you can use Copilot to rewrite existing text in Word. You can use this same functionality in Teams.

Unlike Word, Copilot can't draft *new* text for you in Teams. You must first type your message as normal. However, instead of hitting the *send* icon when you're finished, click the **Copilot** icon in the action bar.

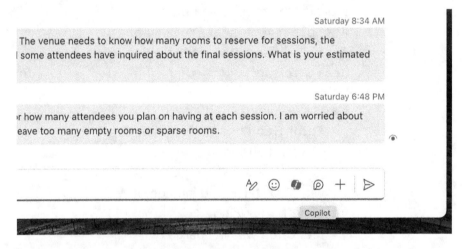

Figure 9-16. *The message action bar contains a Copilot icon for rewriting text*

For this example, I have a delicate situation in which I must be more firm and clear with a coworker who is taking too long to complete a task. I'm not sure how to word it for clarity, and I don't think my tone is appropriate. Let's see what Copilot can come up with. I'll type the following text:

We need to get the speaker list finalized
ASAP for FutureTech. The venue has
repeatedly asked how many rooms to hold for
sessions, the program cannot be finished to
go to print, and I've had more than a few
registered attendees ask for the finalized
list of sessions. When do you think you'll
have a finished list for me?

Once you finish typing your message and click the Copilot icon in the action bar, you have two options – **Rewrite**, which will immediately draft a new version of your text, or **Adjust**, which will allow you to choose a desired length and tone.

Figure 9-17. *Click Adjust to choose a desired length and tone of your rewritten text*

In my example, I'll choose **Adjust** and set the tone to be **Professional**. Now I'm ready to click **Rewrite**.

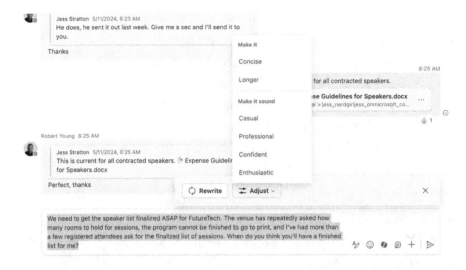

Figure 9-18. Choose a desired length and tone of the rewritten text

Copilot will rewrite my draft. If I like the results, I can click **Replace**, and my old draft will be replaced with the new text. All that's left to do from this point on is click the send icon!

Here's Copilot's version:

> The speaker list for FutureTech is urgent.
> The venue needs to know how many rooms to
> reserve for sessions, the program has to
> be ready for printing, and some attendees
> have inquired about the final sessions. What
> is your estimated timeline for completing
> the list?

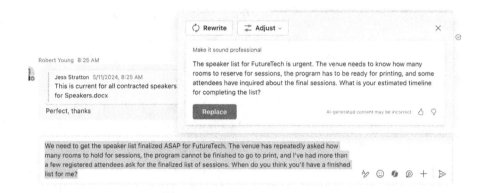

Figure 9-19. *Adjust and rewrite as many times as you like before replacing the desired choice*

One final note – Copilot is a tool that's here for *you*. You can *always* continue to adjust and rewrite until you have a draft you are happy with before replacing your text. Play around with making the text more concise, longer, professional, or more casual until you are confident in what you are sending. Do you only like *some* of Copilot's rewrite? Use that part and change the rest manually with your own words.

Get Questions Answered About Your Organization

You can converse with Copilot directly in Teams using Microsoft Graph-grounded chat. When we used the chat pane in Word, PowerPoint, and Excel, we used it directly related to the specific app we were in – asking for help how to use it, research, or about content in the active document we were working on.

Microsoft Graph-grounded chat lets us ask Copilot about our work, our schedule, and our teammates. I'll go into more detail in the next chapter when I talk about using this on the web, but Teams is an additional dedicated place you can specifically use Graph-grounded chat. I'll also remind you of this in the next chapter.

To access this in Teams, stay in the chat area. You'll see the Copilot icon at the very top above all your existing and pinned chats.

Figure 9-20. Graph-grounded chat is available in the Chat area at the very top of the list

Pin Copilot to the Navigation Bar for One-Click Access

You can also add Copilot to the left navigation bar as an app to access it more quickly.

Clicking the three dots on the navigation bar will bring up a list of Teams apps. Click the Copilot icon, or search for it if it's not there.

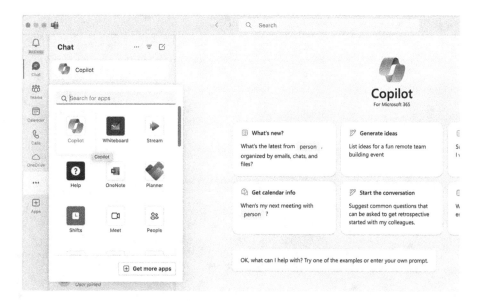

Figure 9-21. *Click the Copilot icon in the apps list to add it to the navigation bar for easy access*

You can pin the app to the navigation bar so it remains even after you reopen Teams. Right-click the Copilot icon and choose **Pin**.

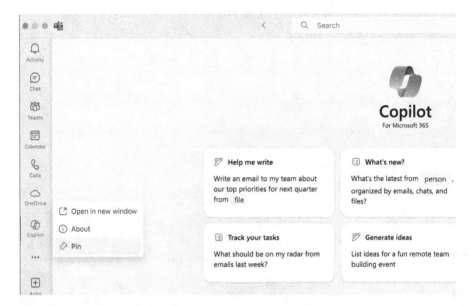

Figure 9-22. *Pin the Copilot icon to the sidebar so it remains there after Teams is reopened*

When you click on Copilot to start a chat, you'll see some suggestions at the top to get you started, and you should notice the **View prompts** button on the bottom right. This will open Copilot Lab where you can see more prompt suggestions you can use.

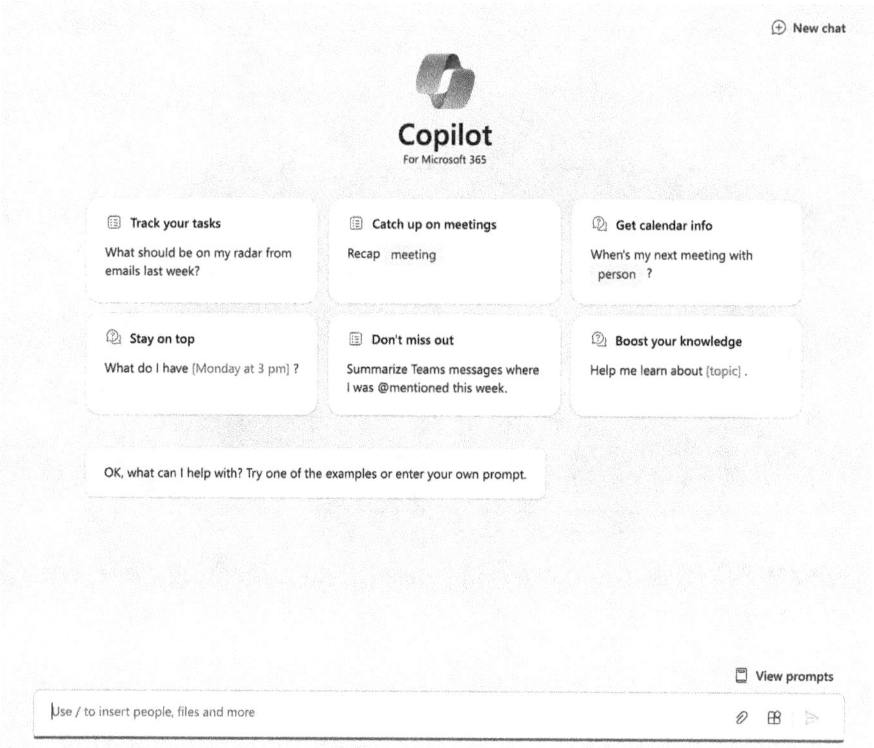

Figure 9-23. *The View prompts button on the bottom right-hand side opens Copilot Lab*

To directly reference or ask about people, files, meetings, and emails, type a / in the prompt area.

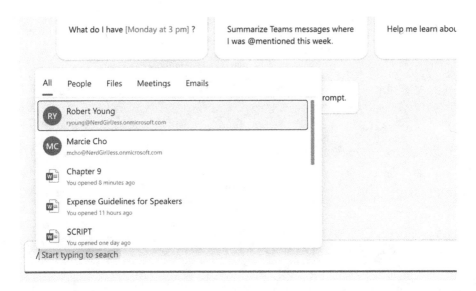

Figure 9-24. *Type a / to reference people, files, meetings, or emails in your prompt*

Figure 9-25. *You can ask questions directly about your organization*

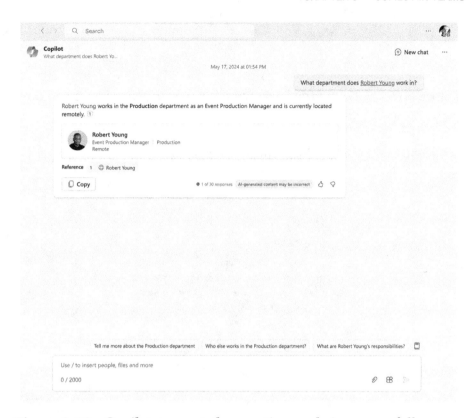

Figure 9-26. *Copilot answers the question and gives some follow-up questions you can also ask*

You can also insert files to use as context by clicking the paperclip icon in the action bar next to the send icon. Clicking this will bring up the identical menu as the forward slash key.

The icon directly next to this is for plugins to use with Copilot, and your network administrator may have different plugins here set up for you to use internally in your organization. The one that I want to focus on here is for turning on web content. Turning on this plugin will enable the ability to use Bing search grounding as part of Copilot's response.

Figure 9-27. *The Plugins icon is directly next to the send icon in the message action bar*

When I click the Plugins icon, I can toggle the switch to turn *on* the web content plugin.

Figure 9-28. *Toggle web content on to use Bing search to enhance Copilot's responses*

What does this mean? Without this toggle, Copilot will return responses from the Microsoft Graph, semantic index, and LLM. If I ask a question about something or someone, it will create its response based on content from documents, emails, and chats that I have access to.

If I enable the web content plugin and ask for more information, Copilot will determine if the quality of the response will be improved by adding results from Bing search. I'm going to talk about that more in depth in the next chapter. For that, we'll move to the web where we can access a dedicated area for a chat with Copilot based on data from your organization's Microsoft Graph, and I'll also show you how you can switch to Copilot with web-grounded chat to take advantage of image creation.

Summary

Copilot in Teams can catch you up and answer questions while you're in a meeting. This is also good for learning what you missed if you need to step away *during* a meeting. To use this feature, the meeting must be transcribed. No one else in the meeting can see the questions you are asking Copilot.

For confidential meetings, you can still use Copilot for use during the meeting to answer questions while not retaining the transcription once the meeting ends. This is a setting in the meeting options. With this setting, Copilot cannot be used to answer questions once the meeting is over.

Without this setting, Copilot can continue to recap and answer questions once the meeting is over by accessing the **Recap** tab in the meeting summary.

Copilot in Teams can also summarize and answer questions about group or individual chat threads, and it can rewrite your messages for better tone and clarity before sending them.

Finally, it can use Microsoft Graph-grounded chat to answer questions about your organization. You can pin the app to the navigation bar for quick access and enable the web content plugin to increase the relevancy and accuracy of Copilot's response.

CHAPTER 10

Copilot in Microsoft Graph-Grounded Chat

I ended the last chapter with a brief discussion on using Graph-grounded chat in Teams, but ultimately kept most of it back so I could focus on it specifically in this chapter. The entire first few chapters of this book gave you valuable introductory knowledge on creating prompts to use in an AI chat experience. That knowledge will culminate in this chapter when we use both web and Microsoft Graph-grounded chat to answer questions not only about life, the universe, and everything but also about the way we work every day.

This chapter is also where two product branches of Copilot converge for you to use. Copilot for Microsoft 365 uses Graph-grounded chat, which we used in Teams at the end of the last chapter. This is a chat that is based on your organization's data. It is possible to include some web grounding to this chat, and I'll be showing you how later.

However, later in the chapter, we'll also be accessing the free Microsoft Copilot to use some of its features. Microsoft Copilot is the same free version I talked about in Chapter 4. Because anyone can use this version of Copilot, it's *only* grounded to the web. Formerly called Bing Chat and Bing Chat Enterprise, these are two separate products. I'll be repeating myself about this a few times, as it's very important to recognize the distinction.

© Jess Stratton 2024
J. Stratton, *Copilot for Microsoft 365*, Inside Copilot,
https://doi.org/10.1007/979-8-8688-0447-2_10

Here's what you can accomplish with Microsoft Graph-grounded chat:

1. Ask questions about your organization, including questions related to your schedule, emails, files, and meetings.

2. Ask general research questions *(with the web content plugin enabled)*.

Here's what you can accomplish with the free Microsoft Copilot's web-grounded chat:

1. Ask general research questions.

2. Ask questions about existing images.

3. Generate images of many artistic styles, such as photorealistic, digital, illustrations, and more.

I'll first finish discussing the remainder of things you can accomplish in Copilot for Microsoft 365 with Graph-grounded chat.

Accessing Graph-Grounded Copilot to Chat

By now you should recognize that Graph-grounded chat means generative AI that's all about your organization. You can chat with Copilot about your schedule, files, teammates, emails, and meetings.

Copilot with Microsoft Graph-grounded chat is accessible via an interface you can get to in the following four ways.

Via the Chat Pane in Microsoft Teams

We finished the last chapter by accessing it in Microsoft Teams. As a quick reminder, you can use Microsoft Graph-grounded chat in Teams by heading to the chat area and clicking **Copilot**, which will be the very top entry, even above your pinned chats.

You may have also pinned it to the navigation bar on the left, for one-click access.

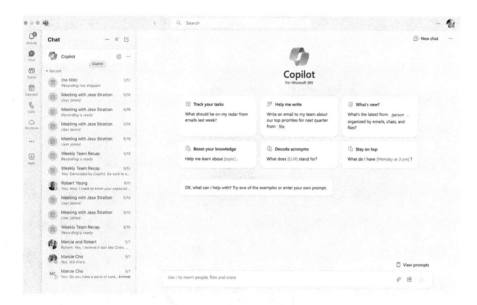

Figure 10-1. *Copilot is accessible in Teams at the top of the chat list*

Via the Copilot Icon on the microsoft365.com Navigation Bar

You can access all the web versions of the apps you use every day on the microsoft365.com portal. After signing in, you can see your recently accessed files along with an app launcher to quickly get to the web versions of apps like Word, Excel, and OneDrive.

On the left-hand side is the navigation bar, containing shortcuts to get to each app quickly. Your apps may vary according to your organization and preferences, but the navigation bar itself is where you'll find the Copilot icon.

Figure 10-2. *The Copilot icon is in the navigation bar on the Microsoft 365 online portal*

The Work Tab at copilot.microsoft.com

These next two methods *also* include a tab to switch to the free web-grounded Microsoft Copilot with commercial data protection, but we're not going to do that just yet.

While the microsoft365.com portal is only available as a generic landing page when not logged in as an existing Microsoft 365 subscriber, *anyone* can access and use the free Microsoft Copilot at copilot.microsoft.com. However, you can also sign in here with your work ID to use Microsoft Graph-grounded chat just as if you were in Teams or the microsoft365.com portal.

As you're a Microsoft 365 user, to use Graph-grounded chat here, you *must* first sign in and then make sure you are on the tab labeled **Work**. This tab won't appear until you've signed in.

The tabs are side by side on the top of the site. In Figure 10-3, you'll see that when you first go to the site and aren't signed in with any account, there are *no* tabs visible and the **Sign in** button is available at the top right. Figure 10-4 shows what it looks like once you're all signed in and have the tabs at the top of the site. We'll switch to the **Web** tab later.

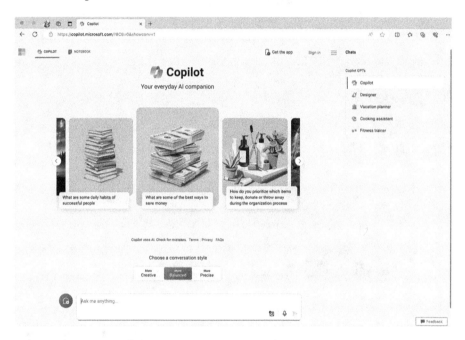

Figure 10-3. *Here's how copilot.microsoft.com looks when not signed in, the Sign in button is visible at the top of the screen and the Work and Web tabs are missing*

Here's the same site when I'm signed in and on the **Work** tab (located at the top):

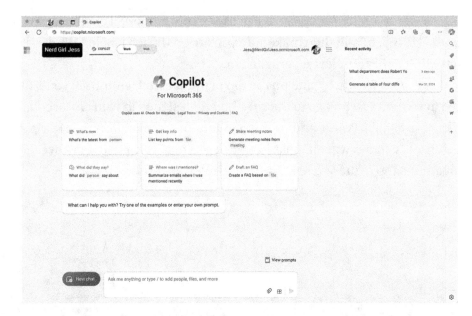

***Figure 10-4.** The same site, signed in with my Microsoft work ID*

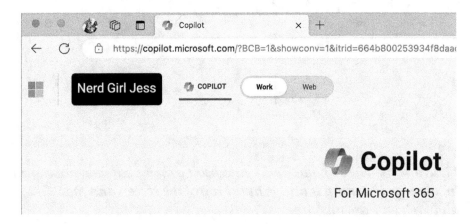

***Figure 10-5.** The Work tab is for Microsoft Graph-grounded chat with your company data; the Web tab is for web-grounded chat with commercial data protection when signed in with your Entra (work) ID*

The Sidebar in the Microsoft Edge Browser

There is one more way you can access Copilot, and it's unique to the Microsoft Edge browser. Edge users can enjoy the special sidebar pane to use Copilot, and you can sign in with your work ID and access the same **Work**/**Web** tabs as the example directly before this one.

Click the Copilot icon on the very top right-hand side of the Edge browser to open the right sidebar pane. You'll be prompted to sign in if you aren't already, and the **Work** tab at the top of the pane will bring you directly to the prompt style you should be very familiar with by now.

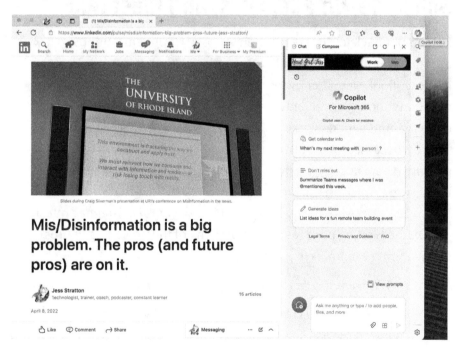

Figure 10-6. *No matter what site you're browsing on Microsoft Edge, click the Copilot icon on the top right-hand side of the browser to open the Copilot pane*

Now that you know the methods of accessing Copilot with Microsoft Graph-grounded chat, let's deep dive into what you can accomplish and how you can get questions answered about your organization. Later in the chapter, I'll switch to the free web-grounded Microsoft Copilot to show you how you can analyze and create images.

Ask Questions About Your Organization, Including Questions Related to Your Schedule, Emails, Files, and Meetings

Remember back in Chapter 8 when we used Copilot in Outlook to ask questions about our emails? I had mentioned that there's no Copilot pane in the Outlook calendar. Instead, *here* is where you can ask all sorts of questions about your schedule with Microsoft Graph-grounded chat. You can ask about your coworkers' schedules, your meetings, and more.

For these examples, I'll be using Copilot with Microsoft Graph-grounded chat at copilot.microsoft.com. Remember, once you're signed in, be sure to click on the **Work** tab at the top of the screen, as shown in Figure 10-5. Here is where you'll be asking all your *work-related* questions.

On the landing page (as shown in many of the preceding figures), you can see some examples to get you started.

> *What emails should be on my radar from last week?*
>
> *What's the latest by [person] organized by emails, chats and files?*
>
> *Provide a comprehensive summary of my emails about [the FY24 Sales Report].*
>
> *Show me any emails from last week where I was @mentioned.*

You can also reference people, files, meetings, and emails by using the / key or clicking the paperclip icon in the prompt area. A list of recently accessed files will appear, but you can manually type a few characters of what or who you're looking for, and your item should appear.

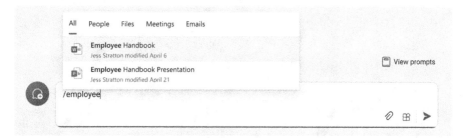

Figure 10-7. *You can reference people, files, meetings, and emails by clicking the paperclip icon or hitting the forward slash (/) key on your keyboard*

I've attached the Employee Handbook we created in Word earlier in the book, and now I'll ask a question about that.

> I'm in the NAMER region. Do we get Memorial
> Day off?

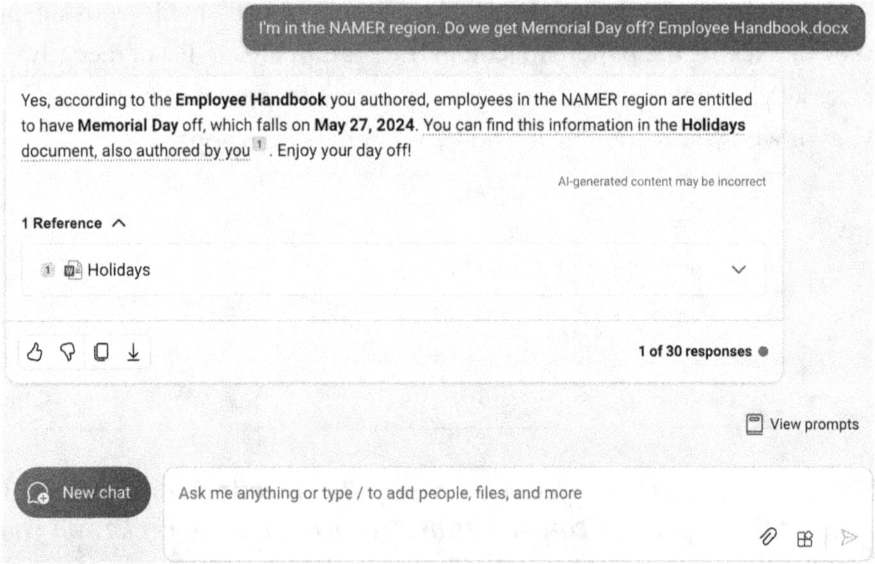

I'm in the NAMER region. Do we get Memorial Day off? Employee Handbook.docx

Yes, according to the **Employee Handbook** you authored, employees in the NAMER region are entitled to have **Memorial Day** off, which falls on **May 27, 2024**. You can find this information in the **Holidays** document, also authored by you [1] . Enjoy your day off!

AI-generated content may be incorrect

1 Reference ∧

1 📄 Holidays   ∨

🖒 🖓 🗐 ↧   1 of 30 responses ●

📖 View prompts

🔾 New chat   Ask me anything or type / to add people, files, and more

📎 🔳 ▷

Figure 10-8. *Copilot answers my question showing me the files it used to get its answer*

The response contains the answer, citations referencing the document, the warning that AI-generated content may be incorrect, a link to the document itself under the **Reference** dropdown, the thumbs-up/thumbs-down button, a link to copy the answer to the clipboard, and a down arrow containing some options to export the response.

I can export the response to a Word document, PDF file, or text document for use elsewhere.

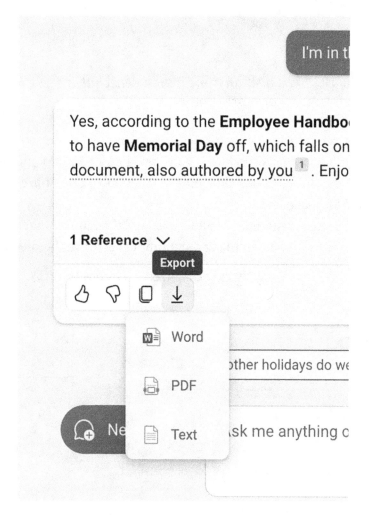

Figure 10-9. *The response can be copied to the clipboard or exported as a Word, PDF, or text file*

You may notice the **1 of 30 responses** in the same dialog box. You can continue chatting about this same topic, adding more context each time. As of this publishing, Copilot can currently respond to the same topic and conversation 30 times, after which it will reset and begin a new chat. You can always click the big blue **New chat** button at any time, which will also reset the chat and let you start over.

Figure 10-10. *Start over anytime with a new chat or reply to give Copilot refinements or more context*

In this example, I'm going to keep going with our existing chat and ask a question about my schedule. Now that I know I have Memorial Day off here in the United States, I'm going to make sure I don't have anything scheduled for that day.

As I can refine with more context, I can use the phrase "that day" and Copilot will know I'm referencing the prompt I used right before it.

Do I have anything scheduled that day?

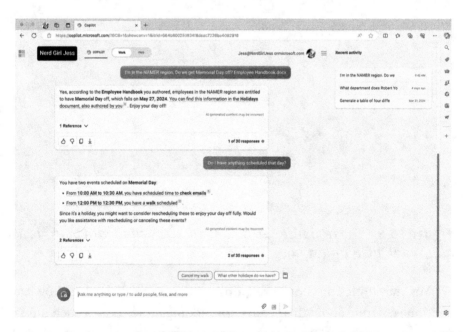

Figure 10-11. *Copilot offers to clear my schedule in response to my prompts*

Copilot looks at my Outlook calendar and tells me I have two appointments that day. Note the response count has incremented to **2 of 30 responses**. I can always fact-check this information by clicking on the citations, and I could type a follow-up prompt to ask for help rescheduling or cancelling the events.

In this case, as shown in the preceding figure, there's a helpful action button in place called **Cancel my walk** that I can click to make it happen right away.

Prepare for Meetings

Remember last chapter when I was late to that meeting about EduCon and other conferences? I now need to update my manager on what we talked about. We went over it in my team's weekly recap meeting and I could always go into the meeting, head over to the **Recap** tab, and look at the summary that Copilot put together for me.

However, I know I can directly reference that meeting in a prompt using the / key and choosing it from the **Meetings** tab. I'll select my Weekly Team Recap meeting and ask Copilot to give me a list of five bullet points to prepare for a meeting with my manager about EduCon.

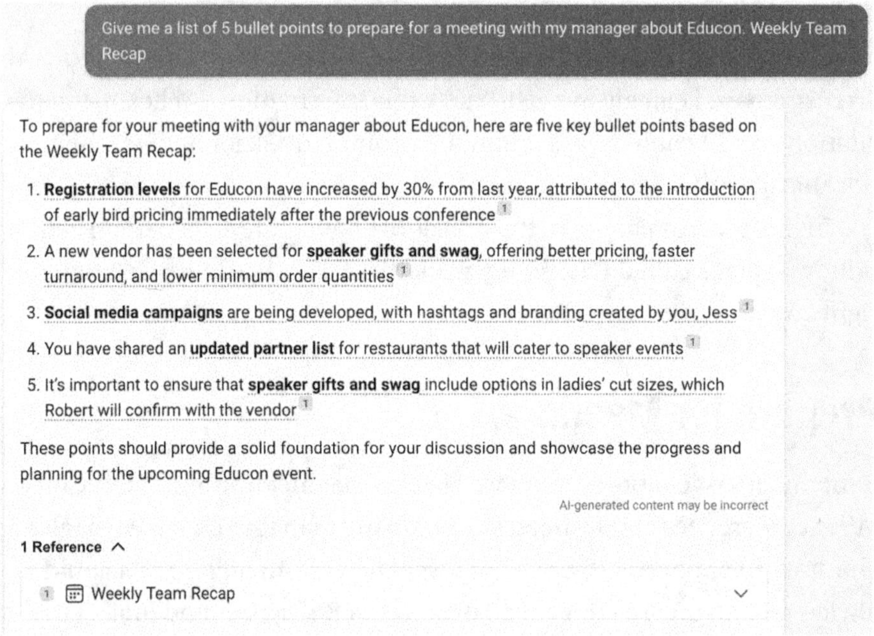

Give me a list of 5 bullet points to prepare for a meeting with my manager about Educon. Weekly Team Recap

To prepare for your meeting with your manager about Educon, here are five key bullet points based on the Weekly Team Recap:

1. **Registration levels** for Educon have increased by 30% from last year, attributed to the introduction of early bird pricing immediately after the previous conference [1]

2. A new vendor has been selected for **speaker gifts and swag**, offering better pricing, faster turnaround, and lower minimum order quantities [1]

3. **Social media campaigns** are being developed, with hashtags and branding created by you, Jess [1]

4. You have shared an **updated partner list** for restaurants that will cater to speaker events [1]

5. It's important to ensure that **speaker gifts and swag** include options in ladies' cut sizes, which Robert will confirm with the vendor [1]

These points should provide a solid foundation for your discussion and showcase the progress and planning for the upcoming Educon event.

AI-generated content may be incorrect

1 Reference ∧

1 ▦ Weekly Team Recap   ∨

Figure 10-12. *Copilot can help prepare for meetings*

As you can see in the preceding figure, Copilot examined my meeting and came up with the main talking points for me.

Use the Web Content Plugin

Your network administrator may have allowed Copilot to reference web content when creating responses to your prompts. This means that Copilot will send special search queries to the Bing search index if accessing current information from the web will help improve the quality and accuracy of the response.

It's important to note that your entire prompt is not being sent over the Internet to a search engine, nor are any documents or files you may have used as references in your prompt. Instead, Copilot will choose the relevant words and phrases from your prompt that will be improved by a web-grounded search.

While your network administrator can *allow* it on their end, you must still *enable* it on your end. When you enable the web content plugin, Copilot will examine your prompt and identify any key terms where an up-to-date web search could improve the quality of the response. Copilot will then take those terms and generate its own search query that it sends to the Bing Search API. This search query is *not* associated with your organization or your specific work sign-in.

If this is something you're comfortable with and think it can enhance your productivity, you can click the Plugins icon in the prompt area and toggle **Web content** to enable it.

Figure 10-13. *Click the Plugins icon in the prompt area to find the web content plugin*

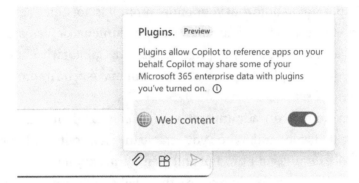

Plugins. Preview

Plugins allow Copilot to reference apps on your
behalf. Copilot may share some of your
Microsoft 365 enterprise data with plugins
you've turned on. ⓘ

🌐 Web content

Figure 10-14. *Toggle the Web content switch to On*

With the web content plugin turned on, I'll ask about The Mariner, a
restaurant I know I've mentioned in Teams before. I would like to know
more about it, so I'll ask Copilot the following:

> What can you tell me about The Mariner
> restaurant?

Now that Copilot is also searching the most current information on
the web, its response contains both data from my organization *and* from
the web and has even categorized them so. You'll see in Figure 10-14 it
has separated them into two sections, **From your company's records** and
From the Web.

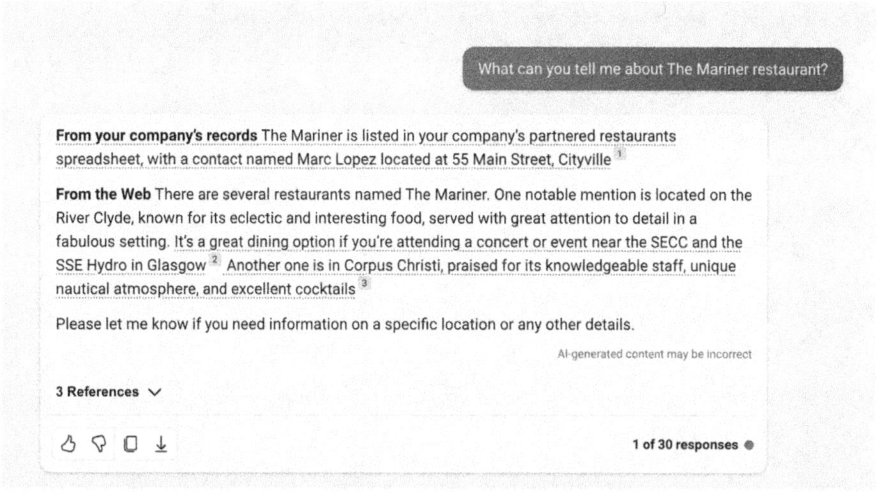

What can you tell me about The Mariner restaurant?

From your company's records The Mariner is listed in your company's partnered restaurants spreadsheet, with a contact named Marc Lopez located at 55 Main Street, Cityville [1]

From the Web There are several restaurants named The Mariner. One notable mention is located on the River Clyde, known for its eclectic and interesting food, served with great attention to detail in a fabulous setting. It's a great dining option if you're attending a concert or event near the SECC and the SSE Hydro in Glasgow [2] Another one is in Corpus Christi, praised for its knowledgeable staff, unique nautical atmosphere, and excellent cocktails [3]

Please let me know if you need information on a specific location or any other details.

AI-generated content may be incorrect

3 References ∨

1 of 30 responses ●

Figure 10-15. *Copilot will now utilize the Bing search index to find additional information*

If I expand **References** to see all the citations, I can see that Copilot has used both internal documents such as an Excel spreadsheet titled "Partnered Restaurants" and two external websites, each linking to a different restaurant called The Mariner. I can further expand the references or click directly on them to go to the source.

Please let me know if you need information on a specific location or any other details.

AI-generated content may be incorrect

3 References ∧

| 1 | 📊 Partnered Restaurants | ∨ |

| 2 | 📄 The Mariner Restaurant | ∨ |

| 3 | 📄 The Mariner, Corpus Christi - Menu, Reviews (18), Photos - Restaurantji | ∨ |

👍 👎 📋 ↓   1 of 30 responses ●

Tell me more about the partnered restaurants spreadsheet   What other restaurants are in Cityville?

What are some other restaurants in Glasgow?

Figure 10-16. *Copilot includes the internal documents and external links it used to form its response*

One final note about the web content plugin. I've mentioned several different ways to get to Copilot with Microsoft Graph-grounded chat, and the plugin is independent to all these methods. If you turn on the web content plugin on the copilot.microsoft.com site, you'll still need to enable it in the chat area of Teams and vice versa.

Analyze Images on Microsoft Copilot's Web-Grounded Chat

So far, we've been using Copilot for Microsoft 365 throughout this entire book, including utilizing the incredibly useful Microsoft Graph-grounded chat. For this last exercise in the book, I'm going to switch over to a different product – Microsoft Copilot. Microsoft Copilot uses a web-grounded chat, meaning it's generative AI that is solely based on web content, not your organization's data (remember, I did warn you I'd be repeating myself. It's that important!).

Using Copilot with web grounding instead of Microsoft Graph grounding means you can use Copilot to ask questions completely unrelated to your work. In fact, you *can't* ask it anything at all about your work files. That's what Microsoft Graph-grounded chat is for! It's for this reason why unlike the microsoft365.com portal, *anyone* can access copilot.microsoft.com and use it for free in a limited fashion.

Up until now we've been on the Work tab. Now, we're going to switch over to the **Web** tab.

Even though we won't be using Graph-grounded chat in this section, and when you visit copilot.microsoft.com you can see the prompt area available to use even when you aren't signed in, it's very important to remember to sign in with your work ID regardless.

Your Copilot for Microsoft 365 license gives you commercial data protection when you use Microsoft Copilot while signed in with your work ID. This means that though Copilot is grounded with the Bing search index instead of your company data, Copilot will *not* retain your previous prompts and responses. It also means that your chats will *not* be used to train the large language models that are used.

Here's a different way I can explain it to really drive home the difference between the two products: When you switch to the **Web** tab, you're switching to a different product called Microsoft Copilot. The benefit of commercial data protection while using Microsoft Copilot is a special perk you get just for being an existing Copilot for Microsoft 365 user.

If you use copilot.microsoft.com without signing in, you won't see those tabs and cannot take advantage of that special commercial data protection.

Why would you even want or need to do this? One reason you might want to switch to the web-grounded Microsoft Copilot is for the ability to analyze and create images, as you cannot accomplish this anywhere in Copilot for Microsoft 365.

To get started, you'll still need to be on <u>copilot.microsoft.com</u> and signed in to view the two tabs, **Work** and **Web**. To analyze images, you'll need to click **Web**.

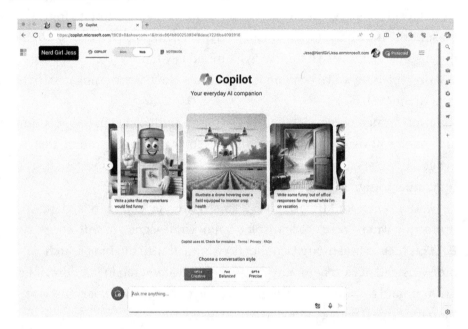

Figure 10-17. *Switching to the Web tab, make sure you are signed in and see the green Protected label next to your sign-in ID and avatar icon*

Be sure to look on the right-hand side of the page to make sure you are signed in, and you see the green **Protected** label next to your sign-in ID and avatar icon.

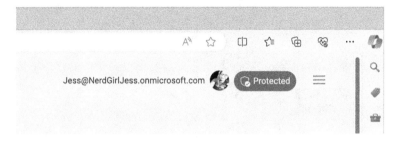

Figure 10-18. *The Protected icon means you are getting Microsoft's commercial data protection*

This screen does look a little different from that of your work Graph-grounded chat. The sample prompts are more general, day to day, and less professional. There are three different choices for responses: **Creative**, **Balanced**, and **Precise**. Those will change both the response length and tone, depending on what you're looking for. It's not as important for analyzing images, but when using it to generate text, it will greatly change the overall tone of the response. I recommend playing around with the three options to become knowledgeable with how the selection changes the response.

Copilot can help you by answering questions about images you can include in your prompt. You can try various questions such as follows:

> *Where is this?*

> *What's in the background?*

> *What breed of [animal] is this?*

> *Where can I buy this?*

To get started, you'll need to share your image with Copilot. Click the image icon in the prompt area (if you hover your mouse over it, you'll see **Add an image**). You can paste an image, upload one from your computer or device, or take a photo with your computer's webcam or mobile phone.

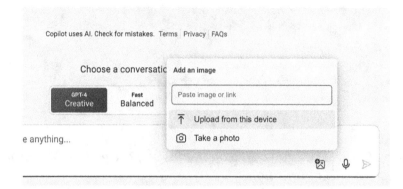

Figure 10-19. *Paste an image or link to an image, upload one from your computer, or take a photo using your computer's webcam*

After adding the image, you can ask Copilot a question about it. I have a picture I took at a fun outing we created for our guest conference speakers. I'd like to do that again, but it was so long ago that I can't remember where it was.

I'll add the image, and then ask Copilot:

    Where is this?

Copilot has successfully identified my image as coming from Pacific Park, the amusement park in the Santa Monica Pier. It's given me direct links to the park, as well as some more sources for me to continue my research.

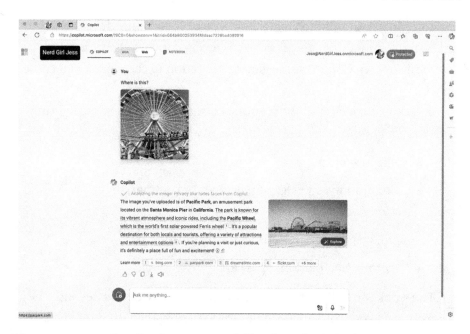

Figure 10-20. *Copilot has successfully identified the location of my photo and given me further research links*

Generate Images Using Copilot Image Creator

You can describe an image you'd like to see, and Copilot can create it for you using OpenAI's DALL-E 3 technology. Formerly called Bing Image Creator, the tool is available in Microsoft Designer and now accessible via the free Microsoft Copilot.

It's once again important to reiterate here that this is *not* directly supported for use within Copilot for Microsoft 365. You can *only* take advantage of image creation by signing in to copilot.microsoft.com with your work ID and switching to the **Web** tab, making sure you see the green **Protected** symbol.

You can ask Copilot to create an image of something, draw something, or illustrate something. You can describe very specifically what you'd like to see or give Copilot some general direction to see what it can come up with.

You can be specific about the subject, scene, style, even the lighting and camera type! You can create images of all sorts of styles:

- Photorealism

- Illustrations such as pencil, charcoal, or marker sketches

- Oil, watercolor, or Renaissance paintings

- Anime, Claymation, or 3D art

The stock photo library for Microsoft 365 subscribers is beyond fantastic, and you can find these photos for use in PowerPoint, Word, and other apps. But sometimes you just need something incredibly specific, or even for use in a social media post. It's those times when you'll want to look to Copilot to create that image for you.

You can start by typing in your prompt just as you would any other. You can make custom art by asking for what you would like to see.

I'm about to send out an email to our employees letting them know that we are retiring a few office printers soon. I'd like to have Copilot create an image for me with a printer that has "retired" and is living it up at a resort by the beach.

I'll give Copilot the following as a prompt:

```
Create an illustration of a laserjet printer
on a beach lounge chair in the sand next to
the ocean at sunset. There is a table with a
Mai Tai on it with an umbrella straw.
```

Copilot will produce four images for me to choose from and some additional text below that I might want to use to refine my image. In this example, it's given me exactly what I was looking for and even suggested I might want to add some seagulls, or a hammock.

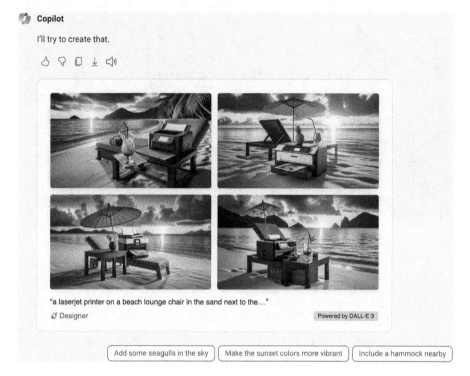

Figure 10-21. *Copilot gives me four image choices and some refinement suggestions*

I can choose an image by clicking on it. It takes me to a larger version of the image, plus a description and the Content Credentials of the image, where it's disclosed that the image was generated with AI. From here, I can right-click the image to save it to my computer to insert it into an email, Word document, PowerPoint presentation, or wherever I need it.

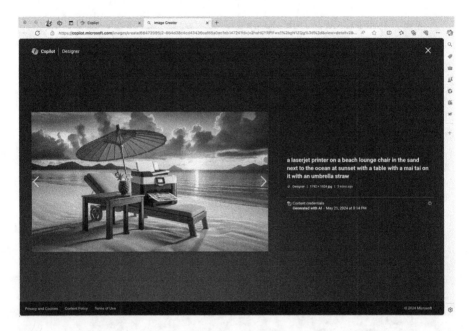

Figure 10-22. *I can download the photo, and the Content Credentials will be included as image metadata to disclose that the image was generated with AI*

Content Credentials is part of the Azure OpenAI service. It's a tamper-evident system to verify that the image was created and generated by DALL-E 3 and a timestamp of when the image was created. These credentials are based on specifications from the Coalition for Content Provenance and Authenticity (C2PA), and it's cryptographically signed by a certificate belonging to the Azure OpenAI service. These measures were created to build trust around AI-generated images.

If you have an image you'd like to check the credentials of, you can upload it to the Content Credentials Verify website at `https://contentcredentials.org/verify`.

Microsoft has a fantastic AI prompting guide, complete with inspiration and tips on how to make a comprehensive prompt to get the most specific image you can envision. You can find the guide at `www.microsoft.com/en-us/bing/do-more-with-ai/ai-art-prompting-guide`.

We did it! Together, we've explored what Copilot can do in Microsoft Word, PowerPoint, Excel, Outlook, Teams, and Graph-grounded chat and even played with creating images in the free Microsoft Copilot (with web-grounded chat). Up next, I'll tidy the book up nice and neat with a very brief outline of the Copilot ecosystem across Microsoft.

Summary

Copilot with Microsoft Graph-grounded chat is accessible in several places including Teams, the microsoft365.com web portal, and copilot.microsoft.com (after signing in with your Work ID and making sure you're on the **Work** tab). Graph-grounded chat is specific and unique to Copilot for Microsoft 365 as it is directly related to your organization.

Here, you can ask questions about your organization, including questions related to your schedule, emails, files, and meetings. You can also ask general research questions and get additional accuracy and relevancy to your responses by enabling the web content plugin.

Your Copilot for Microsoft 365 license also enables you to be able to use the free web-grounded Microsoft Copilot while benefitting from commercial data protection. This is also accessible via copilot.microsoft.com; however, after signing in with your Work ID, you must change to the **Web** tab. Here you can ask questions about existing images, and you can create your own images. You need to switch to the Web tab to specifically use Microsoft Copilot to accomplish this as image creation and analysis is not supported in Copilot for Microsoft 365.

Microsoft Copilot is a separate product from Copilot for Microsoft 365. You cannot analyze or create images as part of Copilot for Microsoft 365. Microsoft Copilot utilizes web-grounded chat for Internet-based responses, while Copilot for Microsoft 365 uses Microsoft Graph grounding to enable you to ask questions specific to your organization. This is an important distinction.

CHAPTER 11

A (Brief) Talk About Copilot in the Microsoft Ecosystem

We made it! As we move into the concluding chapter of this journey we've taken together, let's take a moment to appreciate the new knowledge you've gained. Aside from learning about how to use Copilot for Microsoft 365 directly within those apps, you've also learned a bit about the history of generative AI as well as how to construct a basic prompt.

It's worth a mention that for the mere cost of this book and the time it's taken you to read it, you've just helped make yourself incredibly more marketable, opened yourself up to new career opportunities, and have given yourself a competitive edge in a rapidly paced technology race.

Not only that, but learning how to fully leverage Copilot within the Microsoft apps will save you time *every single day*. If computing and processing power is the currency of AI, then time is the new currency of workers today. You'll be managing time better, creating content faster, and analyzing data more efficiently.

© Jess Stratton 2024
J. Stratton, *Copilot for Microsoft 365*, Inside Copilot,
https://doi.org/10.1007/979-8-8688-0447-2_11

I want to end with a (brief) discussion about what you can do to move forward and continue your journey experiencing and learning about artificial intelligence in more Microsoft products.

Copilot Is a Brand

In Chapter 4 when I talked about accessing Copilot, I itemized the many product versions of Copilot, including the free publicly available version. This was not the first product to be released in the Copilot family brand.

That honor would go to GitHub Copilot. Acquired by Microsoft in 2018, GitHub continues to operate independently as a platform for developers to collaborate on software apps together.

OpenAI, GitHub, and Microsoft collaborated themselves to provide an artificial intelligence model that was trained on billions of lines of open-source code. The end result means that chatting in natural language about coding can rapidly increase the workflows of developers who use GitHub.

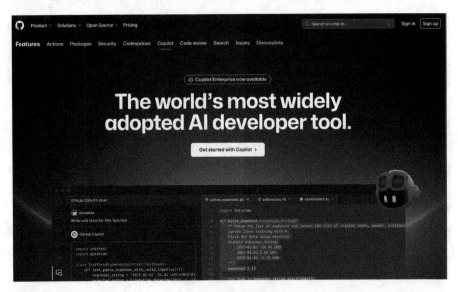

Figure 11-1. *GitHub Copilot now even has an enterprise edition for developers*

Here's just a small list of some tasks developers use GitHub Copilot for:

- Asking questions about how to accomplish tasks like responsive design in web development

- Troubleshooting bugs in their software

- Generating code in numerous programming languages

- Improving old, outdated code

- Assisting code reviewers in explaining why they made code changes

The Brand Becomes Unified Across Microsoft Products

Microsoft Copilot as a generative AI tool was introduced and previously titled Bing Chat, then the more secure Bing Chat Enterprise, available only in the Bing search engine and the Microsoft Edge web browser. The Copilot titling came with the announcement of its integration into the Microsoft 365 suite of apps, along with a new logo for Copilot.

Shortly after, Microsoft announced it would be integrating a product called Windows Copilot into Windows 11, replacing the previous voice assistant Cortana. It would not be long until Microsoft made the decision to rebrand all Copilot products to the full name of *Microsoft Copilot* with the same unified logo across each product.

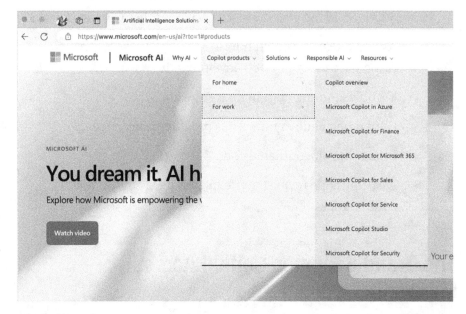

Figure 11-2. *The list of Microsoft Copilot products is expanding at a rapid pace*

Microsoft Copilot in Windows

Copilot in Windows is currently being rolled out to Windows 11 users in both preview mode and via Windows Update. Accessible by clicking **Windows+C** or using the Copilot in Windows icon on the taskbar, you can sign in using your Microsoft account or Microsoft Entra work sign-in.

Figure 11-3. *Copilot appears in preview mode in the Windows 11 taskbar*

Copilot in Windows will appear on the right side as a pane, both the location and interface you are familiar with. It can also respond to all the prompts you are familiar with, with a few additions that are specific to the Windows operating system.

Copilot in Windows can switch from light to dark mode, turn on do not disturb mode for you, and open apps. It can mute your speakers and notifications, take screenshots, and even troubleshoot devices that aren't working.

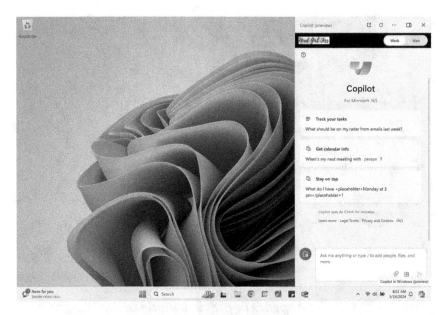

Figure 11-4. *Copilot when logged in with Entra ID on the work tab*

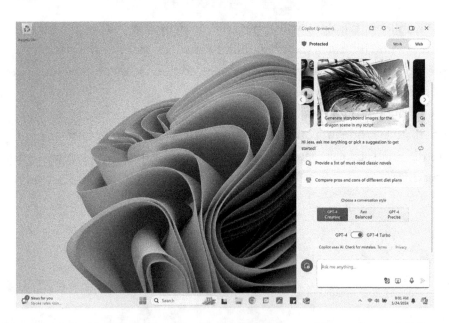

Figure 11-5. *Copilot when logged in with Entra ID on the web tab, note the Protected icon*

Copilot Gets Its Own Key

Just before this publishing, Microsoft announced a new initiative called Copilot+ PCs. Certain brands and models of PCs, laptops, and tablets will come out of the factory with Microsoft Copilot in Windows and the beefy computing power needed to handle it, along with a dedicated Copilot key on the keyboard to activate the sidebar pane.

Devices include Microsoft Surface and other OEM partners such as Acer, ASUS, Dell, HP, Lenovo, and Samsung computers, laptops, and tablets, though you'll have to check each model individually for inclusion.

Microsoft Copilot for Finance

Microsoft is rapidly expanding products available using the incredible artificial intelligence that is based on Microsoft Copilot technology. Currently in preview is Microsoft Copilot for Finance, a product designed for finance professionals. Connecting directly to Microsoft Excel and other financial tools such as ERP, users can get assistance with repetitive tasks, gain insights, and use analytic tools.

Copilot for Finance utilizes AI-generated reconciliation to quickly find missing transactions, analyze variances, and integrates with Outlook to access customer and ERP records right from within the app.

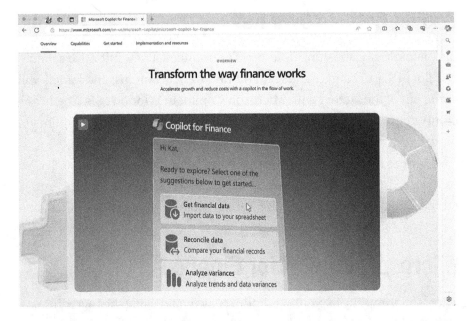

Figure 11-6. Microsoft Copilot for Finance, as advertised on the web

Microsoft Copilot for Service

Up next in the product lineup is for customer service agents and the customers they serve. Microsoft Copilot for Service integrates directly into existing CRM solutions instead of requiring a separate installation. These integrations include Outlook and Teams, where users can enjoy service-specific tailored responses and prompt abilities to provide better service to customers.

Outlook can draft emails about relevant case summaries that are obtained from CRM records and can even add contacts directly to the CRM. Teams can also update CRM records while your meetings are in progress!

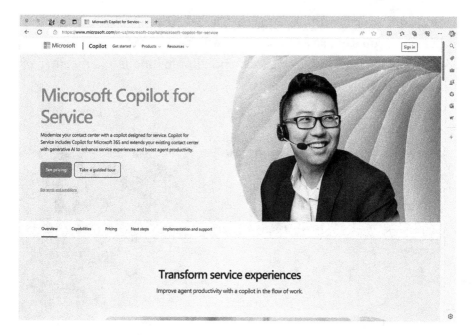

Figure 11-7. *There's also a site landing page for Microsoft Copilot for Service*

Microsoft Copilot for Sales

One of the earliest branches of Copilot in the Microsoft ecosystem, Copilot for Sales, has been available since February 2024. This seller-specific AI brings its own unique tools and insights specific to the sales industry. Users can create sales pitches and analyze sales calls directly from Microsoft Teams.

Integrating directly with Microsoft Dynamics 365 Sales and Salesforce Sales Cloud, information can be shared seamlessly between the Microsoft 365 apps you use every day.

Industry-specific Copilot apps such as Sales become incredibly useful when you can use AI to perform tasks that previously had to be done manually, such as looking for competitor mentions in a meeting, or generate keywords for promotions.

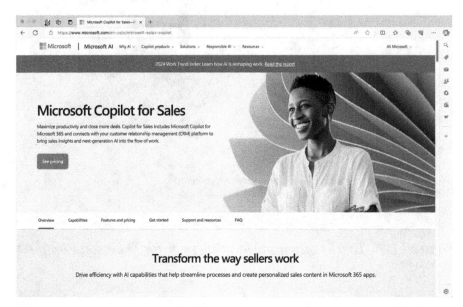

Figure 11-8. *Microsoft Copilot for Sales was one of the first products to branch out*

Microsoft Copilot for Security

So far, we've seen industry-specific products for sales, finance, and service professionals. What about the unsung heroes that run the servers that let them do their jobs? I'm talking about the network administrators and network security professionals. In the name of transparency, I will disclose my own bias here as I was one myself many years ago!

There's so much going on behind the scenes to make things run smoothly; our industry joke is that our existence is only known when things go wrong. Fortunately, we now have one more tool to help things safe for you.

Microsoft Copilot for Security provides natural language assistance as it does in the other mentioned products and just like Copilot in Microsoft 365. It's available as a standalone experience at `https://securitycopilot.microsoft.com` or embedded into other Microsoft products seamlessly, such as Microsoft Defender XDR, Defender Threat Intelligence, and Intune, and third-party services such as ServiceNow.

Copilot for Security can summarize incidents, reverse engineer malware scripts, analyze the possible impact of incidents, and provide guided responses when incidents happen. These responses include directions to assist administrators on investigating the incident as well as containing it.

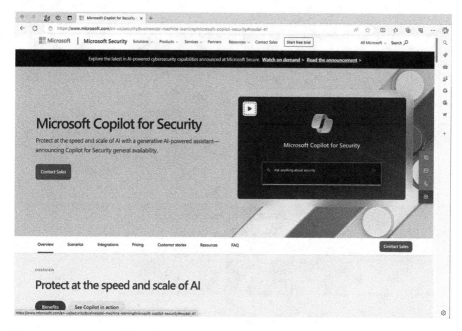

Figure 11-9. *Copilot for Security is one of the few products that uses a standalone app*

Microsoft Copilot Studio

I've saved my favorite for last – Copilot in Microsoft 365 can be customized for the exact specific needs of your organization. This customization comes in the form of creating your own copilot experience in Microsoft Copilot Studio.

What does that mean? Your HR department can release an employee self-service chat portal to answer questions specific to the HR policies of your company. Your customer service team can add a customer self-service chat directly to your public website.

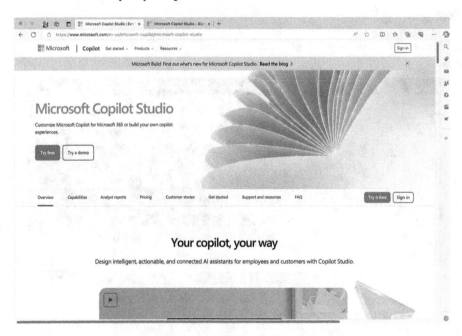

Figure 11-10. *Copilot Studio comes with Copilot for Microsoft 365*

These custom copilots can be added as an app for your employees and teammates in Microsoft Teams, or added to other non-Microsoft company-specific apps you may use.

The copilots can be triggered by *events*, not prompts.

One final note on Copilot Studio – these copilots can even be created by prompt. You can tell Copilot Studio what kind of copilot you are looking to create, and it will get you started. Whether it's an employee onboarding process, IT help desk ticket workflow, or inventory management, you can create it with Microsoft Copilot Studio.

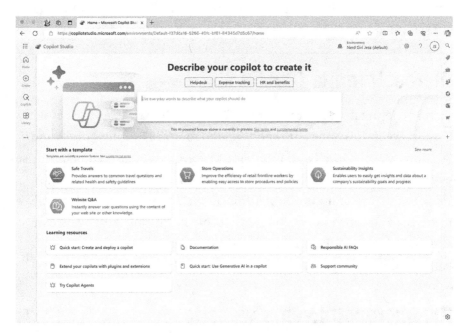

Figure 11-11. *Use a prompt to create your own copilots*

The Future of Microsoft Copilot

This heading is a bit misleading as I cannot know the future any more than anyone else, but what I *do* know is where to look to find out what Microsoft has planned for us, both upcoming and newly released.

There are two big Microsoft conferences held yearly, and Microsoft nearly always plans its big software release announcements around these. Even if you don't attend, you can always find the recaps and news headlines of any big announcements made during these conferences.

Microsoft Build

Microsoft Build is an annual conference geared toward developers. Focused on developing technology for apps and services, this conference features keynotes and sessions dedicated on discussing the future of technology and artificial intelligence. You can find out more information and see video highlights from the event at `https://build.microsoft.com`.

Microsoft Ignite

Microsoft Ignite is another major conference held yearly. As Microsoft's flagship event, this one is primarily geared toward IT professionals and decision makers as well as developers. The event is focused on enterprise-level products and technology, so while Microsoft Build is an event to watch out for major news about artificial intelligence, Microsoft usually makes big announcements about Microsoft 365 during Ignite. You can learn more about Ignite on the official web page at `https://ignite.microsoft.com`.

The Microsoft Events Website

You can find out about every event Microsoft has planned at their events portal website. This includes both in-person conferences like Build and Ignite as well as virtual events that anyone can register for and attend. The site contains events and dates and even categorizes them by specific target roles. You can find and browse the full event catalog at `www.microsoft.com/events`.

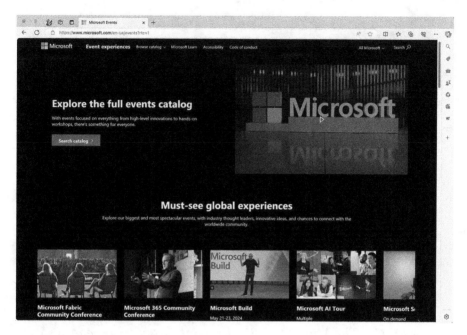

Figure 11-12. *The Microsoft Events site contains dates of every event you can attend, both in-person and virtual*

The Microsoft 365 Blog

Did you know that each Microsoft product has a blog that's updated regularly? Each article contains new features as well as tips and tricks on using the product more productively. I highly recommend bookmarking the Microsoft 365 blog and setting time aside on your calendar to scroll through and see what's new each month. *Hint: Ask Copilot Graph-grounded chat to find the best time for you to do this once a month!*

It's easy to switch the category to a specific app, so you can also narrow down the blog to articles about Excel, Microsoft Copilot for Microsoft 365, and even Windows 11-specific articles.

The blog can be found at `www.microsoft.com/microsoft-365/blog`.

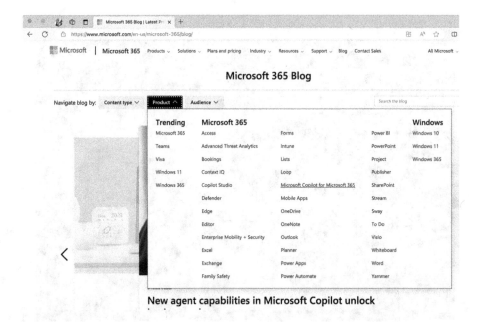

New agent capabilities in Microsoft Copilot unlock

Figure 11-13. *The Microsoft 365 blog contains entry categories, including one on Copilot*

Don't Stop Learning!

At LinkedIn Learning, my previous employer that I now contract for, we have a saying – *always be learning*. By reading this book, you're partaking in the very spirit we thrive on, and now I'm going to encourage you to continue. Generative AI is here to stay, and sites, products, and solutions are growing at a rapid pace. Read the blogs. Watch the press events. Learn the technology. It's here to help you.

I'm also here to help you. Once again, my name is Jess Stratton, and if you have any questions, you can find me on the LinkedIn platform at www. linkedin.com/in/nerdgirljess or on my website at www.nerdgirljess. com. If you follow me on LinkedIn, I announce when I do live events or have some great tips to share. Even if you don't have any questions, I'd love to hear your favorite features of Copilot in Microsoft 365, or a neat way you've found to use it.

Speaking of using it, the more you use Copilot, the better you'll understand what it can do. There's no way that I could mention every possible use for it simply because I do not know what repetitive tasks or problems you need to solve daily. If Copilot can't do something, it will tell you.

I would love to end this book waxing poetic about the paradigm shift artificial intelligence is causing in how we work, learn, and use technology to assist with our daily lives. But to do so would delay you the ability to simply *get out there and use it.*

I thought it would be fun to ask Microsoft Copilot directly for some advice for you if you're just getting started. Here's what it had to say.

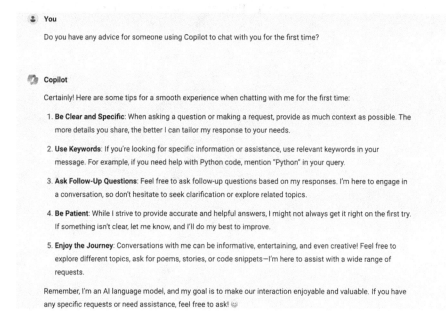

Figure 11-14. *Who better than to ask how to use Copilot, than Copilot itself?*

So what are you waiting for? Go, sign in, and start chatting.

Summary

Copilot is a brand. GitHub Copilot was the first product in the family, as a partnership between OpenAI, GitHub, and Microsoft. Now there are many products in the family, including Copilots to help with sales, service, IT support, and the finance industry.

You can even create your own copilots with Copilot Studio. With the ability to create copilots from a prompt, you can customize it to fit the specific needs of your organization.

To keep up to date with Microsoft and AI advancements, you can attend or watch highlights from their two biggest conferences, Build and Ignite. You can also attend virtual events directly from the Microsoft Events site. Finally, make time to read the Microsoft 365 blog to get updates about Copilot in Microsoft 365 or even to find out what's new in your favorite app.

Index

A, B

Application programming interface
(API), 29
Artificial intelligence (AI), 4, 35, 37
feedback mechanism, 40
generative AI, 41–45
Responsible AI
(*see* Responsible AI)
safety consideration, 39
thumbs-up/down
mechanism, 40

C, D

Chat AI technology, 3, 7, 9, 19, 26
ChatGPT, 5–8, 16, 18, 25–27, 41
Clippy, 20, 21, 35
Copilot, 19
branches, 49
brand, 242
GitHub, 242
list tasks, 243
unified logo across, 243, 244
Build services, 254
business/enterprise, 62–65
installation, 63
subscriptions, 64

verification, 64, 65
Clippy, 20
command bars, 19
commercial data protection, 28
Copilot Pro (*see* Copilot Pro)
customer service agents,
248, 249
definition, 49
ecosystem, 241
elements, 27
event website, 254, 255
Excel (*see* Excel workbook)
finance professionals, 247, 248
Graph, 29, 30
grounding process, 30
conceptual
understanding, 32
Graph-grounded chat, 31
web grounding, 31, 32
Ignite, 254
Internet connection, 22–24
large language models, 27
LinkedIn Learning, 256, 257
Microsoft 365, 34, 35, 49, 56
apps, 33, 34
blog and setting, 255, 256
business customers, 56

© Jess Stratton 2024
J. Stratton, *Copilot for Microsoft 365*, Inside Copilot,
https://doi.org/10.1007/979-8-8688-0447-2

E, F

G, H

I, J, K

L

GPSR Compliance
The European Union's (EU) General Product Safety Regulation (GPSR) is a set
of rules that requires consumer products to be safe and our obligations to
ensure this.

If you have any concerns about our products, you can contact us on

ProductSafety@springernature.com

In case Publisher is established outside the EU, the EU authorized
representative is:

Springer Nature Customer Service Center GmbH
Europaplatz 3
69115 Heidelberg, Germany